This book is from

the kitchen library of

_____

_____

# Mr. Food®'s Good Times, Good Food Cookbook

### Art Ginsburg
**Mr. Food®**

WILLIAM MORROW AND COMPANY, INC.

NEW YORK

Library of Congress Cataloging-in-Publication Data
Ginsburg, Art.
        Mr. Food's good times, good food cookbook   /   Art Ginsburg.
            p.      cm.
        ISBN 0-688-16777-2
        1. Cookery.   I. Title.
    TX714.G5714   1999
    641.5—dc21                                                    99-13368
                                                                   CIP

Printed in the United States of America

First Edition

1   2   3   4   5   6   7   8   9   10

BOOK DESIGN BY MICHAEL MENDELSOHN OF MM DESIGN 2000, INC.

www.williammorrow.com
www.mrfood.com

DEDICATED TO

*my family and friends*
*for making and sharing*
*the good times and good food with me*

# Acknowledgments

When we think about good times in our lives, sure, we think about the holidays and special occasions, but we also think about the day-to-day experiences we've had with those special people who are always around for us. Good times don't come just with planned events like weddings and graduations, but also, and maybe even more importantly, with simple times like heart-to-heart chats over lunch, or those warm smiles and pats on the back we get just when we need them the most. That's why it's so important to me to thank the wonderful team that not only has been essential in putting this book together, but also helps create *my* good times and good food.

There are the managers who keep an eye on my books and other projects, Howard Rosenthal and Caryl Ginsburg Fantel, who always jump in with just the right idea when I need it, along with their assistants, Larissa Lalka and Rhonda Weiss, who keep track of the many important details.

Joining me in my test kitchen to share lots of chuckles and plenty of great suggestions are Patty Rosenthal, Janice Bruce, Cheryl Gerber, Cela Goodhue, and Gerri Seinberg, along with Joe Peppi, who oversees all the work done in my test kitchen. Thanks to all of you and also to Dio Gomez, who makes sure that our kitchen always has its good-feeling sparkle. Thanks, guys!

Since one of the best parts of having good times is sharing them with people you like, I want to thank my other dedicated managers—Steve Ginsburg, Chet Rosenbaum, and Tom Palombo—and office staff—

# Acknowledgments

Carol Ginsburg, Alice Palombo, Heidi Triveri, Beth Ives, and Robin Steiner—who take care of business for me by coordinating everything with our 170-plus TV stations, keeping track of our finances, and working with food councils and companies from around the country. Marilyn Ruderman, my asssistant, keeps me organized so I have enough time to work on new recipes *and* visit all the cities and fans I love so much, while Helayne Rosenblum, my script assistant, always helps me find just the perfect words. My wife, Ethel, continues to be there for me to share more good times than I could ever list. And, of course, my son Chuck and the rest of my family are always on hand with their invaluable encouragement, too!

Yes, these people are my friends, family, and my extended family, along with others who offer their never-ending support, from my agent, Bill Adler, to all the people at publisher William Morrow, especially Bill Wright, President and CEO of the Hearst Book Group; Michael Murphy, Publisher and Senior Vice President; Senior Editor Zachary Schisgal; Art Director Richard Aquan; Nikki Basilone, Vice President and Director of Special Sales; Patrick Jennings, Special Sales Manager; and, of course, my terrific book designer, Michael Mendelsohn of MM Design 2000, Inc.

I could never forget to thank my circle of friends at QVC, who are always encouraging me to come out with new books and to share them with their viewers. It's such a pleasure to work with Karen Fonner, Paula Piercy, and everyone else at QVC!

Wow! What a lucky guy I am, because all these folks I've just thanked, plus you, my loyal readers and viewers, are the people who share with me the days that make up the good times, the good food, and, of course, all the "OOH IT'S SO GOOD!!®"

# Contents

Acknowledgments     vii

Introduction     xi

A Note About Packaged Foods     xiii

Awesome Appetizers     1

Swingin' Soups, Salads, and Dressings     13

Snazzy Breads, Sandwiches, Pizzas,
    and More     33

Chart-Toppin' Poultry     51

Outta-Sight Meats     65

Far-out Fish and Seafood     79

Groovy Vegetables     91

Peachy-Keen Potatoes, Rice, and Noodles     107

Dazzlin' Desserts     127

Be-boppin' Beverages     157

Index     171

# *Introduction*

My original idea for this book was to re-create the great foods of the 1950s, as well as share some tasty nostalgia. Let's face it, those of us who are old enough to remember the '50s know that it was a time when people knew how to have fun. We'd listen to that "rebellious" rock 'n' roll music on the jukebox at the local soda fountain and watch the latest comedy shows on our new televisions. And it seemed that everything we did had food tied in with it.

So you see, it really made perfect sense for me to do a cookbook about those great times and the foods we loved then. And once I started organizing my ideas, I had loads of fun remembering things like my favorite episodes of *I Love Lucy* and the first time I heard Elvis. Of course, the memories of my favorite meals brought a smile to my face, too. Boy, those *were* the days.

So I brought the idea to my offices and test kitchen. Everybody thought the recipes were great, but they didn't all share my enthusiasm for the memories of the '50s. I guess that's because nostalgia means different things to different people. Since my staff come from different parts of the country and range in age from their mid-twenties to sixty-plus, it's natural that our cultural and personal memories vary quite a bit. And that's the way it is with you, my readers, too. While some of us remember twisting to the songs of Chubby Checker, others might remember Saturday nights spent learning how to do the hustle or dancing to the disco hits of the 1970s. In fact, the youngest members of my staff are the ones really enjoying swing music and dancing now . . . for the *first* time! So, you see, I realized that even though our favorite TV shows, music, and teen idols may be different, one thing's for sure—we've all had 'em.

Another thing we all have in common is fond memories of favorite foods enjoyed in particular settings. Whether our favorite memory is of nights at the downtown pizza hangout chomping on piping-hot pizza, pancake breakfasts at the local community center, or dinners of comfort foods like meat loaf and mashed potatoes made with love and served in our own kitchen by Mom, we all have food memories that make us feel warm and cozy inside.

Some people say "the good old days" were the best ones, while others say now is the best time. That's what this cookbook is all about—foods that evoke or make memories. It's a mix of favorites from yesterday made with shortcuts of today. For a tasty blast from the past, some recipes follow those slow-cooking techniques our moms and grandmas used, but they're easier than ever—I promise.

Yup, there's everything here from Oniony Finger Bread, Chicken Potpie, Mom's Pot Roast, and Surprise Gravy to Crazy Carrot Salad, Maple Turkey Sausage, and Special Creamed Spinach. Now don't think I'd forget dessert! It's super-satisfying and memorable when you've got choices like Blueberry Betty, Mile-High Chocolate Malted, Strawberry Rhubarb Pie, and Shortcut German Chocolate Cake. Nobody will be able to resist these yummy tastes of yesterday!

So whether you're 15 or 95—or anywhere in between—you're gonna love this book, 'cause it's got something for everybody: yummy recipes, fun facts, easy hints and tips, and, of course, a whole bunch of "OOH IT'S SO GOOD!!®"

# A Note About Packaged Foods

Packaged food sizes may vary by brand. Generally, the sizes indi-
cated in these recipes are average sizes. If you can't find the exact
package size listed in the ingredients, whatever package is closest in
size will usually do the trick.

# Mr. Food®'s Good Times, Good Food Cookbook

# Awesome Appetizers

Grilled Vegetables with Onion Dip — 3
Mash 'Em, Smash 'Em Guacamole — 4
Crispy Crunchy Pita Chips — 5
Party Pâté — 6
Rockin' Rollin' Cheese Ball — 7
Memory Lane Antipasto — 8
Anytime Deviled Eggs — 9
Sweet-and-Sour Wings — 10
Creamy Fruit Cup — 11

# Grilled Vegetables with Onion Dip

Something old, something new . . . yup, here I've replaced traditional crunchy dipping veggies with today-popular grilled veggies to serve with a dip that was a favorite of yesterday: packaged onion soup mix and sour cream. That means we've got a winner every time we serve it!

    1 container (16 ounces) light sour cream
    1 envelope (1 ounce) onion soup mix
    2 large yellow squash, cut into sticks
    2 bell peppers (1 each red and green), cut into 1-inch strips
    1 medium zucchini, cut into sticks
    1 tablespoon olive oil
    ¼ teaspoon salt
    ¼ teaspoon black pepper

In a medium bowl, combine the sour cream and soup mix; mix well. Cover and chill until ready to use. In a large bowl, combine the remaining ingredients; mix well. Heat a grill pan or skillet over high heat. Grill the vegetables in batches for 5 to 6 minutes, or until lightly browned but still crisp. Allow to cool slightly before serving, or chill; serve with the onion dip.

# Mash 'Em, Smash 'Em Guacamole

---

### about 2 cups

---

In the '60s and '70s, guacamole was typically made by mashing fresh ripe avocados. It's more popular than ever today, and we have our choice of premade packages and mixes at the supermarket. Those are great, but when I've got the time, I'll always go back to the way we made it in "the olden days" for the real thing.

> 2 large ripe avocados, halved, pitted, and peeled
> ¼ cup salsa
> 1 tablespoon fresh lemon juice
> 1 teaspoon salt

In a medium bowl, mash the avocados with a fork until chunky. Add the remaining ingredients; mix well. Serve, or cover and chill until ready to serve.

**Note:** Serve with tortilla chips or Crispy Crunchy Pita Chips (opposite page). Before storing this in the refrigerator, cover it with plastic wrap and press the plastic wrap against the surface of the dip. That'll prevent the guacamole from turning brown.

# Crispy Crunchy Pita Chips

---

### *8 dozen chips*

---

It used to be that you could find exotic appetizers and side dishes like hummus and baba ghanoush only in ethnic food stores. Fortunately for us, nowadays Mediterranean and Middle Eastern foods are easy to find in our local supermarkets. So why not bake up a few homemade chips to enjoy 'em all with?

Six 6-inch pita breads
½ cup (1 stick) butter, melted
¼ cup grated Parmesan cheese
1 tablespoon dried oregano
1 teaspoon garlic powder

Preheat the oven to 350°F. Cut each pita bread into 8 equal wedges and separate each wedge into 2 pieces. In a medium bowl, combine the remaining ingredients; mix well. Place the pita wedges rough side up in a single layer on large rimmed baking sheets. Brush each wedge evenly with the butter mixture. Bake for 6 to 8 minutes, or until golden and crisp. Allow to cool, then serve, or store in an airtight container until ready to serve.

*Note:* To add extra color and zing, sprinkle the chips with ground red pepper before baking. And don't worry, these can be made up to a couple of days ahead of time, so you can always have them on hand.

# Party Pâté

## about 2¼ cups

At one time, chopped chicken liver was considered a particularly ethnic dish. Not anymore! These days, the trendy variation is called pâté, and it's as "hot" as can be.

1 tablespoon butter
1 pound chicken livers
1 small onion, chopped
3 hard-boiled eggs
½ teaspoon salt
¼ teaspoon ground red pepper
¼ cup heavy cream

Melt the butter in a medium skillet over medium-high heat. Add the chicken livers and onion and sauté for 8 to 10 minutes, or until the livers are cooked through. Allow to cool slightly, then place in a food processor that has been fitted with its metal cutting blade; add the hard-boiled eggs, salt, and ground red pepper, then process until smooth. While processing, slowly pour the cream through the feed tube until the mixture is smooth. Transfer to a serving bowl, cover, and chill for at least 2 hours before serving.

*Note:* What a perfect dish to prepare ahead of time! Sprinkle it with some chopped parsley and serve with crackers.

# Rockin' Rollin' Cheese Ball

Cheese balls never go out of style. That's probably because they're a tried-and-true, tasty classic. And nowadays, if we're watching our waistlines, it's easy to lighten up our cheese balls . . . just like this!

>  ¼ cup finely chopped fresh parsley
>  1 package (8 ounces) light pasteurized processed cheese spread, softened
>  4 ounces light cream cheese, softened
>  ½ teaspoon dry mustard
>  ⅛ teaspoon ground red pepper

Place the parsley in a shallow dish. In a medium bowl, beat the remaining ingredients until well blended. Shape the mixture into a ball, then roll in the parsley, coating completely. Serve, or wrap well and chill until ready to serve.

**Note:** It's fun to have themed parties, and this dish gives us a way to carry over our rock 'n' roll—or any other—theme onto the hors d'oeuvre table. Just form it into the shape of a musical note or any other simple shape that fits the party.

# Memory Lane Antipasto

*4 to 6 servings*

Remember the first time the family sat around the table and shared a big antipasto? What tasty memories! And now it's easier than ever to re-create them, 'cause the freshest authentic Italian ingredients are available right in our local supermarkets. There's no need to run around to specialty stores to find just what we want for our special family salad.

> 1 medium head iceberg lettuce, cut into bite-sized pieces
> ¼ pound thinly sliced ham, tightly rolled or cut into ½-inch strips
> ¼ pound thinly sliced Genoa or other hard salami, folded in half or quartered
> ½ pound fresh mozzarella cheese, cut into 1-inch chunks
> 2 medium tomatoes, cut into chunks
> 1 jar (6 ounces) marinated artichoke hearts, drained
> 1 jar (7 ounces) roasted peppers, drained and cut into ½-inch strips
> 12 peperoncini
> 1½ cups extra-large pitted black olives (about 20 olives), drained
> ½ cup Italian dressing

Cover the bottom of a large platter with the lettuce. Arrange the ham, salami, cheese, tomatoes, artichoke hearts, roasted peppers, peperoncini, and olives over the lettuce. Pour the dressing over the salad and serve.

*Note:* Sometimes I like to prepare individual plates of this antipasto and keep them chilled until guests arrive. If you do that, instead of topping them with dressing as instructed above, drizzle it over each salad just before serving.

# Anytime Deviled Eggs

---
## 1 dozen deviled eggs
---

One thing's for sure, from our great-grandparents' day to ours, deviled eggs are a family favorite that never goes out of style. And whether we serve 'em at a fancy cocktail get-together or a backyard picnic, they're always the hit of the party.

> 6 eggs
> 3 tablespoons mayonnaise
> 1 teaspoon yellow mustard
> ⅛ teaspoon sugar
> ⅛ teaspoon salt
> ⅛ teaspoon ground red pepper, plus extra for garnish

Place the eggs in a small saucepan and add enough water to cover them. Bring to a boil over high heat; remove the pan from the heat, cover, and allow to sit for 20 minutes. Drain the hot water and run cold water over the eggs. Allow to cool for 5 to 10 minutes, then peel. Slice the eggs lengthwise in half and remove the yolks. In a medium bowl, combine the egg yolks, mayonnaise, mustard, sugar, salt, and ⅛ teaspoon ground red pepper; mix well. Spoon the mixture back into the egg whites. Serve immediately, or cover and chill until ready to serve. Sprinkle the tops with ground red pepper.

## Did You Know . . .

while some families pass down recipes, others pass down show biz fame? First Ozzie and Harriet Nelson starred in their popular TV show in the '50s and '60s, son Ricky topped the music charts in '58, and his own twin sons, Gunnar and Matthew, did the same in 1990, known simply as Nelson!

# Sweet-and-Sour Wings

*4 to 6 servings*

It wasn't so long ago that the only place we could find flavorful chicken wings was in a Chinese restaurant. Things have sure changed, 'cause they're in big demand today. As an appetizer, snack, or even dinner, wings are an anytime spicy-hot or sweet-and-tangy favorite.

1 package (2½ pounds) frozen split chicken wings, thawed
½ cup sweet-and-sour sauce
¼ cup teriyaki sauce
2 tablespoons sesame seeds

Preheat the oven to 450°F. Coat a rimmed baking sheet with nonstick cooking spray. Place the chicken wings on the baking sheet and bake for 20 minutes. Remove from the oven; drain off the fat from the pan if necessary. In a large bowl, combine the remaining ingredients. Add the chicken wings; toss to coat well. Place the coated wings back on the baking sheet; brush with any remaining sauce and return to the oven. Bake for 8 to 10 minutes per side, or until the glaze begins to caramelize and no pink remains in the chicken. Serve immediately.

**Note:** There are many varieties of sweet-and-sour sauce, so, depending on the type you use, the flavor of your wings will vary. (Szechwan duck sauce and others like it can be very spicy.)

# Creamy Fruit Cup

There's nothing like a fruit cup, especially when it's made with really fresh ingredients. Sure, we can buy canned or frozen fruit, but every once in a while it's nice to take an extra step to get that fresh-picked taste. And when it's served with this creamy dressing . . . mmm!

> 1 can (6 ounces) pineapple juice
> 1 package (3 ounces) cream cheese
> 2 tablespoons sugar
> 1 teaspoon grated orange peel
> ¼ cup orange juice
> 2 teaspoons cornstarch
> 1 pint strawberries, washed, hulled, and sliced
> 2 red apples, cored and cut into chunks
> 2 pears, cored and cut into chunks
> 2 bananas, peeled and sliced (see Note)

In a medium saucepan, combine the pineapple juice, cream cheese, sugar, and orange peel over medium heat; mix well and cook until smooth, stirring occasionally. Pour into a medium bowl. In a small bowl, combine the orange juice and cornstarch; mix well and stir into the cream cheese mixture, stirring until thickened. Cover and refrigerate until cold. Place the remaining ingredients in a serving bowl or individual bowls. Drizzle with the sauce and serve.

***Note:*** Bananas tend to turn dark quickly once they're cut, so drizzle them with a little lemon juice to slow down that process—or simply cut and add the bananas to the rest of the fruit just before serving.

# Swingin' Soups, Salads, and Dressings

| | |
|---|---|
| Cream of Pimiento Soup | 15 |
| Voilà Vichyssoise | 16 |
| Velvety Corn Soup | 17 |
| Onion Ring Salad | 18 |
| Tomato-Lover's Salad | 19 |
| Wedged Salad | 20 |
| Chop-Chop Salad | 21 |
| Refrigerator Layered Salad | 22 |
| Italian Veggie Toss | 23 |
| Confetti Zucchini Salad | 24 |
| Timeless Garden Salad | 25 |
| Crunchy Cucumber Salad | 26 |
| Crazy Carrot Salad | 27 |
| Old-fashioned Coleslaw | 28 |
| Carrot and Pineapple Mold | 29 |
| "Baked" Potato Salad | 30 |
| French Vinaigrette | 31 |

# Cream of Pimiento Soup

Slang sure does change with the times. What we called "groovy" or "hip" years ago might be "phat" or "awesome" today. The names of foods change, too—for instance, the pimientos of yesterday are now usually referred to as roasted peppers. It doesn't matter to me what they're called, 'cause they sure do taste good, especially as part of this creamy soup.

> 2 cups milk
> 1 can (10½ ounces) condensed chicken broth
> 1 jar (7½ ounces) pimientos, drained
> ½ small onion, quartered
> 3 tablespoons butter, softened
> ¼ cup all-purpose flour
> ½ teaspoon black pepper

Place all the ingredients in a blender and blend until smooth. Pour into a large saucepan and heat the mixture over medium-high heat until it reaches a boil, stirring frequently. Cook for 2 to 3 minutes, or until the soup is smooth and slightly thickened, stirring constantly. Serve immediately.

*Note:* To make your soup look extra-special, top each serving with some chopped fresh parsley and a thin slice of lemon.

# Voilà Vichyssoise

It may have a French name, but vichyssoise was actually created in New York City. This creamy cold potato soup is a refreshing, elegant way to get everybody's appetite ready for the great meal that's sure to follow!

2 tablespoons butter
2 large onions, chopped
2 cans (14½ ounces each) ready-to-use chicken broth
3 large potatoes, peeled and thinly sliced
1 rib celery, thinly sliced
¼ teaspoon salt
¼ teaspoon white pepper
2 cups (1 pint) half-and-half
1 cup milk

Melt the butter in a large saucepan over medium heat. Add the onions and cook for 8 to 10 minutes, or until tender. Add the chicken broth, potatoes, celery, salt, and pepper; mix well. Bring to a boil; cover and boil for 10 to 12 minutes, or until the potatoes are tender. Pour into a bowl and refrigerate the mixture for at least 2 hours, or until well chilled. Place the potato mixture in a blender and blend on high speed until smooth. Pour into a serving bowl and add the half-and-half and milk; mix well. Serve, or cover and chill until ready to serve.

*Note:* Chopped scallions are the perfect colorful topper to add just before serving.

# Velvety Corn Soup

Remember how when you were a kid, the choice of soups at most Chinese restaurants was limited to one or two selections? Well, that's not so anymore! Here's one of the new ones that's become very popular in Chinese restaurants around the country . . . and your homemade version is guaranteed to be a winner, too!

> 2 cans (14½ ounces each) ready-to-use chicken broth
> 2 cans (14¾ ounces each) creamed corn
> ¼ teaspoon black pepper
> 1 tablespoon water
> 2 teaspoons cornstarch
> 1 egg, beaten
> 2 scallions, thinly sliced

In a large saucepan, combine the chicken broth, creamed corn, and pepper; bring to a boil over medium-high heat. In a small bowl, combine the water and cornstarch, stirring until smooth. Add to the broth mixture and simmer for 2 to 3 minutes, or until slightly thickened, stirring occasionally. Swirl the beaten egg slowly into the soup, forming thin strands. Serve topped with sliced scallions.

***Note:*** Yes, it's okay to make the soup in advance and simply reheat when ready to serve.

# Onion Ring Salad

The burger boom of the '50s also introduced another rage that's still popular today: crispy batter-fried onion rings. I bet you'll be the first one on your block to serve 'em like this . . . and start a new rage!

1 package (20 ounces) frozen French-fried onion rings
½ cup creamy Caesar dressing
2 tablespoons real bacon bits
1 large head romaine lettuce, cut into bite-sized pieces

Bake the onion rings according to the package directions; let cool slightly. In a small bowl, combine the dressing and bacon bits; mix well. Place the lettuce on a large serving platter. Drizzle with the dressing mixture and top with the onion rings. Serve.

## Did You Know . . .

Although the term *fast food* dates back to the 1950s, it was not until the '60s that restaurants like McDonald's, Burger King, Pizza Hut, Wendy's, Arby's, Kentucky Fried Chicken, and others became popular.

# Tomato-Lover's Salad

At one time, vine-ripened tomatoes were available only during certain seasons. For a tomato lover like me, the off-seasons were hard times. It's a good thing that today we can get them practically all year long. This salad is just one yummy way to celebrate.

⅓ cup vegetable oil
2 tablespoons red wine vinegar
2 tablespoons chopped fresh parsley
½ teaspoon dried oregano
¼ teaspoon dry mustard
¼ teaspoon salt
¼ teaspoon black pepper
2 large tomatoes, thinly sliced
1 large onion, thinly sliced and separated into rings

In a large bowl, combine the oil, vinegar, parsley, oregano, mustard, salt, and pepper; mix well. Add the tomatoes and onion; toss to coat well. Cover and chill for at least 2 hours before serving.

***Note:*** Serve individual portions of this salad on iceberg lettuce leaves. They not only add color, they also keep the dressing from running into the other foods on the plate.

# Wedged Salad

Isn't it funny how sometimes we can remember something that happened years ago but not something that happened this morning? Well, when I was putting together this chapter, a vivid memory popped into my head—it was of the iceberg lettuce wedges my wife always used to serve topped with a zippy sour cream dressing. I couldn't wait to try it again—and I can't wait for you to try it, too!

1 cup sour cream
¼ cup milk
1 tablespoon prepared white horseradish
1 tablespoon fresh lemon juice
1 teaspoon grated onion
½ teaspoon dry mustard
½ teaspoon paprika
½ teaspoon salt
1 medium head iceberg lettuce, cut into 6 wedges
1 small carrot, grated

In a medium bowl, combine all the ingredients except the lettuce and carrot; whisk until well blended. Place each lettuce wedge on a salad plate. Drizzle with the dressing and sprinkle with the grated carrot. Serve immediately.

***Note:*** Of course, this dressing can be made ahead and stored in the fridge for a few days before serving.

# Chop-Chop Salad

Can you imagine how much work this must have been years ago? Today, with our mini food processors and electric choppers, we can have this one on the table in no time!

¼ cup vegetable oil
3 tablespoons cider vinegar
1 tablespoon chopped fresh mint
1 teaspoon sugar
½ teaspoon garlic powder
¼ teaspoon dried oregano
½ teaspoon salt
¼ teaspoon black pepper
2 cucumbers, seeded and finely diced (see Note)
1 large tomato, seeded and finely diced
1 small onion, finely diced

In a medium bowl, combine the oil, vinegar, mint, sugar, garlic powder, oregano, salt, and pepper; mix well. Add the remaining ingredients; toss to mix well. Cover and chill for at least 1 hour before serving.

**Note:** To seed a cucumber, just slice it in half lengthwise, then scoop out the seeds with a melon baller or a spoon. And while you're at it, why not hollow out some tomatoes to serve this in? Then you'll have a side dish that's also a pretty, edible garnish.

# Refrigerator Layered Salad

What do I mean by a layered salad? Here's what—a bunch of colorful vegetable layers topped with a mayonnaise dressing that accents the fresh taste of the veggies. Got it? (You really *should* get some!)

   1½ cups mayonnaise
   1 tablespoon sugar
   1 teaspoon curry powder
   1 medium head iceberg lettuce, shredded
   2 large tomatoes, chopped
   ½ pound fresh mushrooms, sliced
   1 medium red onion, thinly sliced and separated into rings
   10 radishes, sliced
   1½ cups (6 ounces) shredded Swiss cheese
   ¼ cup real bacon bits

In a small bowl, combine the mayonnaise, sugar, and curry powder; mix well and set aside. In a large glass serving bowl, layer the lettuce, tomatoes, mushrooms, onion rings, radishes, cheese, and bacon bits. Spread the dressing over the top; cover and chill for at least 2 hours, or overnight, before serving. Toss and serve.

***Note:*** The nice thing about this salad is that it can be made a day ahead of time, so there's no last-minute chopping and preparation.

# Italian Veggie Toss

When I started looking for older recipes that are better than ever now, this quick salad idea came across my desk. It's simple to make, and oh, what a kick it's got!

    1 bottle (8 ounces) Italian dressing
    1 teaspoon cayenne pepper sauce
    1 tablespoon sugar
    1 can (14 ounces) artichoke hearts, drained and quartered
    ½ pound fresh mushrooms, halved (see Note)
    1 medium red onion, thinly sliced and separated into rings

In a large bowl, combine the dressing, cayenne pepper sauce, and sugar; mix well. Add the remaining ingredients; toss to mix well. Cover and chill for at least 2 hours before serving.

***Note:*** Options, options, options! You can substitute 2 drained 4-ounce cans of button mushrooms for the fresh mushrooms, if you'd like.

# Confetti Zucchini Salad

*4 to 6 servings*

Boy, do I love checking out what's available at the local farm stand. Living in Florida, I get to do that . . . often! Yup, there's nothing better than crunching into fresh veggies. No matter where you live and what time of year it is, this salad has all the freshness you'd ever want to remind you of farm-fresh summer produce.

> 3 medium zucchini, thinly sliced (see Note)
> 2 ribs celery, finely chopped
> 1 medium red bell pepper, finely chopped
> 1 medium yellow bell pepper, coarsely chopped
> 2 tablespoons chopped fresh parsley
> ½ cup Italian dressing
> 1 tablespoon sugar

In a large bowl, combine the zucchini, celery, bell peppers, and parsley; mix well. In a small bowl, combine the dressing and sugar; mix well. Pour over the vegetable mixture and toss to coat evenly. Serve, or cover and chill until ready to serve.

***Note:*** The easiest way to thinly slice the zucchini is to use a food processor with a slicing disc.

# Timeless Garden Salad

When you're in a pickle for a quick tossed salad that'll please the whole gang, break out the iceberg and mix up this one. It'll be dressed and ready to go in no time!

    1 cup mayonnaise
    ½ cup ketchup
    ½ cup sweet pickle relish, drained
    1 medium head iceberg lettuce, cut into bite-sized pieces
    1 large tomato, cut into wedges
    1 medium cucumber, thinly sliced

In a medium bowl, combine the mayonnaise, ketchup, and relish; mix well. Place the lettuce in a salad bowl and top with the tomato wedges and cucumber slices. Drizzle with the dressing, toss, and serve.

***Note:*** It's no problem to prepare the dressing ahead of time and chill it until ready to use.

# Crunchy Cucumber Salad

This trick of soaking cucumbers in ice water to make them extra-crispy is one I learned from my mom. I passed it on to my kids and now they have their own kids, who think these cukes are the best ever!

2 medium cucumbers, peeled and thinly sliced
1 tablespoon salt
3 cups ice water
4 scallions, thinly sliced
½ small red bell pepper, chopped
¼ cup sour cream
2 tablespoons white vinegar
2 tablespoons sugar
¼ teaspoon black pepper

In a large bowl, combine the cucumbers, salt, and ice water. Cover and chill for 1 hour; drain and return the cucumbers to the bowl. Add the remaining ingredients and mix until well combined. Cover and chill for at least 2 hours before serving.

*Note:* I like to peel the cucumbers for this salad, but you can also use them unpeeled, or run a fork down the skins before slicing to give them a ridged look.

# Crazy Carrot Salad

You've gotta admit that over the years, some pretty bizarre food combinations have been popular. I'm talking about dishes that are actually tasty but sound so strange it's hard to get ourselves to try them. Here's one. It dates back quite a few years, yet it's still around—'cause it's a true classic. See for yourself.

> 6 medium carrots (about 1 pound), shredded
> ½ cup raisins
> ¾ cup mayonnaise
> 1 teaspoon sugar
> 1 small head iceberg lettuce, shredded

In a large bowl, combine all the ingredients except the lettuce; mix well. Place the lettuce on a platter and spoon the carrot mixture over the top. Serve immediately, or chill until ready to serve.

***Note:*** For a contemporary twist, you might want to substitute sweetened dried cranberries for the raisins, and you could use baby spinach leaves in place of the shredded lettuce.

# Old-fashioned Coleslaw

Remember when making homemade coleslaw meant getting out the hand grater? Well, today's convenient packaged coleslaw mixes let us say good-bye to scraped knuckles. Why, all the shredded vegetable combinations available at the supermarket help us enjoy our favorite homemade coleslaw taste in half the time.

½ cup mayonnaise
2 tablespoons milk
2 tablespoons sugar
1 tablespoon yellow mustard
2 teaspoons white vinegar
½ teaspoon salt
½ teaspoon black pepper
1 package (16 ounces) shredded coleslaw mix (see Note)
1 medium green bell pepper, diced

In a large bowl, combine the mayonnaise, milk, sugar, mustard, vinegar, salt, and pepper; mix well. Add the coleslaw mix and green pepper; toss to mix well. Serve immediately, or cover and chill until ready to serve.

*Note:* Sure, you can shred your own cabbage, if you'd prefer. About 4 cups of it, with a little shredded carrot for color, will take the place of the packaged mix here.

# Carrot and Pineapple Mold

---

## 4 to 6 servings

---

Back in the '50s, gelatin salads were all the rage. Anything and everything was mixed with flavored gelatin to make interesting concoctions. So why not put a 45 on the record player—or should I say pop a CD into the stereo system?!—and get back into that spirit with this tasty tribute to the past.

> 2 cans (8 ounces each) crushed pineapple, drained,
>     with juice reserved
> ½ cup water
> 1 package (4-serving size) lemon-flavored gelatin
> 3 large carrots, grated

In a medium saucepan, bring the reserved pineapple juice and the water to a boil over high heat. Remove from the heat and add the gelatin; stir until dissolved. Add the grated carrots and the pineapple; mix well. Pour into a 1-quart gelatin mold; cover and chill for at least 4 hours, or until firm. Unmold onto a serving platter and serve.

## Did You Know . . .

Even though it first became hip to Shake, Rattle 'n' Roll with that radical dessert called Jell-O in the 1950s, the jiggly stuff was actually invented all the way back in 1897?!

# "Baked" Potato Salad

Potluck dinners are a timeless way to get together and share food and fun with friends, and potato salad always seems to be at the top of everybody's must-have list. Well, this time, you're gonna be sure to walk in with the trendy and tasty dinner winner that tastes as good as our favorite dinnertime baked potatoes.

> 8 medium potatoes (about 3 pounds), scrubbed and
>     cut into 1-inch chunks
> 1 tablespoon salt
> 1 container (16 ounces) sour cream
> ¼ cup real bacon bits
> 4 scallions, thinly sliced
> ½ teaspoon black pepper

Place the potatoes in a large pot and add enough water to cover them. Add the salt and bring to a boil over high heat. Cook for 10 to 15 minutes, or until fork-tender; drain well and allow to cool slightly. In a large bowl, combine the remaining ingredients; mix well. Add the potatoes and mix until well combined. Serve warm, or cover and chill until ready to serve.

*Note:* For a really loaded "baked" potato salad, add 1 cup (4 ounces) shredded Cheddar cheese along with the sour cream and other ingredients.

# French Vinaigrette

Today if we're offered French dressing, we think of a tangy orange one. But that wasn't always so. You see, in the days of poodle skirts and bobby socks, French dressing was more what we think of now as vinaigrette-style, like this flavor-packed one.

⅓ cup olive oil
⅓ cup red wine vinegar
2 teaspoons dried basil
½ teaspoon sugar
½ teaspoon garlic powder
½ teaspoon salt
½ teaspoon black pepper

In a small bowl, whisk the oil, vinegar, basil, sugar, garlic powder, salt, and pepper until well blended. Use immediately, or cover and chill until ready to serve.

*Note:* For simplicity and convenience, serve this over packaged mixed salad greens. That way, all the work of cutting and cleaning is already done for you.

# Snazzy Breads, Sandwiches, Pizzas, and More

| | |
|---|---|
| Muffin Tin Cloverleaf Rolls | 35 |
| Parmesan Garlic Rolls | 36 |
| Crispy Buttery Biscuits | 37 |
| Sour Cream Muffins | 38 |
| Old-time Corn Bread Muffins | 39 |
| Oniony Finger Bread | 40 |
| All-Wrapped-Up Garlic Bread | 41 |
| Mom's Cheese Melts | 42 |
| "Souper" Burgers | 43 |
| Bubblin' Beer Dogs | 44 |
| Beefed-Up Chili Sauce | 45 |
| Veggie-Packed Pizza | 46 |
| Homemade Pizza Sauce | 47 |
| Stack-'Em-Up Chocolate Chip Pancakes | 48 |
| Walnut Maple Syrup | 49 |

# Muffin Tin Cloverleaf Rolls

Poor Grandma! To make her homemade rolls, it took hours of mixing, kneading, and proofing. Today we're lucky—we can use convenience items like frozen bread dough. So that leaves us with extra time to call Grandma and thank her for all the love she poured into everything she made for us.

> 2 tablespoons butter, melted
> 1 teaspoon dried dillweed
> 1 pound frozen bread dough, thawed and cut into
>     18 pieces (see Note)

Coat a 6-cup muffin tin with nonstick cooking spray. In a medium bowl, combine the butter and dillweed; mix well. Dip the dough pieces one at a time into the butter mixture and place 3 in each muffin cup. Cover and allow to rise at room temperature for about 40 minutes, until doubled in size. Preheat the oven to 375°F. Bake the rolls for 20 to 25 minutes, or until golden brown. Serve warm.

**Note:** Make sure to plan ahead when you want to make these. It takes about 1 hour to thaw the bread dough.

# Parmesan Garlic Rolls

Bread sticks and garlic rolls are traditional and tasty starters served at most Italian restaurants. Perfect for dunking in warm spaghetti sauce, they're a great way to take the edge off our appetites before any meal at home, too.

  ¼ cup (½ stick) butter, melted
  ¼ cup grated Parmesan cheese
  1 tablespoon sesame seeds
  ½ teaspoon garlic powder
  1 package (10 ounces) refrigerated bread sticks

Preheat the oven to 375°F. In a medium bowl, combine the butter, Parmesan cheese, sesame seeds, and garlic powder; mix well. Unroll the bread stick dough on a work surface, without separating it into individual bread sticks. Brush half of the butter mixture over the top and roll up again. Separate along the perforations into individual rolls. Coat both sides of each roll with the remaining butter mixture and lay on a rimmed baking sheet. Bake for 12 to 14 minutes, or until golden. Serve warm.

*Note:* Warm some spaghetti sauce for serving along with these as a dipping sauce.

# Crispy Buttery Biscuits

---

## 10 biscuits

---

If you remember the TV classic *Leave It to Beaver,* then you remember seeing June Cleaver always at work in the kitchen making family meals. I bet she would have loved this quick-and-easy recipe back then!

> 1 cup crushed toasted rice cereal
> 1 tablespoon caraway seeds
> 1 package (7½ ounces) any flavor refrigerated biscuits (10 biscuits)
> 3 tablespoons butter, melted

Preheat the oven to 425°F. Coat a baking sheet with nonstick cooking spray. In a small bowl, combine the crushed cereal and the caraway seeds; mix well. Dip each biscuit in the melted butter, then in the cereal mixture, coating completely. Place on the baking sheet and bake for 8 to 10 minutes, or until golden. Serve warm.

## Did You Know . . .

Cheerios, first on the scene in the '40s (and a particular favorite of today's toddlers), were originally called Cheerioats—"the first ready-to-eat oat cereal"?

# Sour Cream Muffins

---

## 6 muffins

---

No matter where on the time line our memory takes us, we've always loved our breads, cakes, and muffins nice and moist. And there's a secret ingredient that guarantees that every time—sour cream!

> 1 cup sour cream
> 1 egg
> 2 tablespoons sugar
> 1 tablespoon butter, melted
> 1⅓ cups all-purpose flour
> 1 teaspoon baking powder
> ½ teaspoon baking soda
> ½ teaspoon salt

Preheat the oven to 400°F. Coat a 6-cup muffin tin with nonstick cooking spray. In a medium bowl, combine the sour cream, egg, sugar, and butter; mix well. Stir in the remaining ingredients until well combined. Spoon equally into the muffin cups and bake for 12 to 15 minutes, or until light golden and a wooden toothpick inserted in the center comes out clean. Serve warm.

***Note:*** For a fancy go-along, combine ½ cup (1 stick) softened butter with 2 thinly sliced scallions and ½ teaspoon garlic powder; mix well. Place on a piece of plastic wrap and form into a log. Chill until firm; remove the plastic wrap and slice into rounds just before serving.

# Old-time Corn Bread Muffins

## 1 dozen muffins

There are times we need to use shortcut mixes and times we don't want to. Want something authentic-tasting that's easy to make even without a packaged mix? Got it right here!

1½ cups milk
⅓ cup vegetable oil
1 egg
2 cups yellow cornmeal
1 cup all-purpose flour
3 tablespoons sugar
1 tablespoon baking powder
1 teaspoon salt

Preheat the oven to 425°F. Coat a 12-cup muffin tin with nonstick cooking spray. In a large bowl, combine all the ingredients; mix well. Spoon the batter into the muffin cups and bake for 18 to 20 minutes, or until golden. Serve warm.

**Note:** Stir a bit of honey into some whipped butter to make a special old-fashioned country spread for serving with these.

# Oniony Finger Bread

At one time or another, we've all enjoyed a hearty portion of spoon bread. A cross between bread and pudding, it's traditionally eaten with a spoon . . . hence the name. I call this one oniony finger bread 'cause it's baked like spoon bread, but we can eat it with our fingers.

6 tablespoons butter, divided
2 large onions, thinly sliced
2 cups biscuit baking mix
½ cup milk
1 cup sour cream
1 egg

Preheat the oven to 425°F. Coat an 8-inch square baking dish with nonstick cooking spray. Place 3 tablespoons of the butter in a large skillet over medium-high heat. Sauté the onions for 15 to 20 minutes, or until caramelized. Meanwhile, melt the remaining 3 tablespoons butter; in a large bowl, combine the biscuit baking mix, milk, and the melted butter. Mix well, until a stiff dough forms, then press into the baking dish; cover with the caramelized onions. In a small bowl, combine the sour cream and egg; mix well and pour over the onions. Bake for 20 to 25 minutes, or until the top is set and golden. Allow to cool slightly, then cut and serve warm.

***Note:*** How long you cook the onions depends on how caramelized you like them. I like them very browned, but they're also good lightly sautéed.

# All-Wrapped-Up Garlic Bread

---

## *1 loaf*

---

Cooking in aluminum foil was a real '50s and '60s thing. I'm not sure what made us like it so much—the baked-in taste it gave our foods or the fact that it saved us from having so many pots and pans to wash. Either way, this one's got it all!

    ½ cup (1 stick) butter, softened
    1 garlic clove, minced
    1 tablespoon chopped fresh parsley
    1 loaf (16 ounces) Italian bread, split lengthwise in half
    1 tablespoon grated Parmesan cheese

Preheat the oven to 400°F. In a small bowl, combine the butter, garlic, and parsley; mix well. Spread over the cut sides of the Italian bread, then sprinkle with the cheese. Place the bread halves back together and wrap the loaf tightly in aluminum foil. Bake for 15 to 20 minutes, or until the bread is heated through and crusty. Remove the foil, slice, and serve.

*Note:* This can also be made as individual servings of garlic bread; just slice the bread, spread the garlic mixture on each slice, wrap all the slices together in foil, and bake.

# Mom's Cheese Melts

---
### 12 muffin pizzas
---

I bet you remember having these a lot when you were growing up—'cause they're every mom's version of quick pizza. We loved 'em as kids, and we can love 'em just as much now!

> 6 English muffins, split
> ¼ cup (½ stick) butter, softened
> 2 medium tomatoes, each sliced into six ¼-inch slices
> 12 slices (9 ounces) American cheese

Preheat the broiler. Place the muffin halves cut side up on a cookie sheet. Spread the butter evenly over them. Broil for 2 to 3 minutes, or until the edges begin to brown. Remove from the broiler. Place a tomato slice, then a cheese slice on each half. Broil for 2 to 3 minutes, or until the cheese begins to brown. Remove from the broiler and serve.

***Note:*** Today there are so many sliced cheese choices that we're certainly not limited to American cheese. Why not use Cheddar slices one time, Muenster another, and on and on.

# "Souper" Burgers

*6 servings*

Once flavorful dry soup mixes started showing up on supermarket shelves in the '50s, it didn't take long before creative cooks started adding them to all kinds of recipes. Today, we're still enjoying that "souped up" flavor, like in these juicy onion burgers, shown on the cover!

> 1½ pounds ground beef
> 1 envelope (1 ounce) dry onion soup mix
> 2 tablespoons chopped fresh parsley
> 6 hamburger buns, split and toasted

Preheat the grill to medium heat. In a large bowl, combine all the ingredients except the buns; mix well. Form into 6 equal-sized patties. Grill for 4 to 5 minutes per side, or until the juices run clear and no pink remains. Serve on the buns.

*Note:* Why not give these "souper" burgers a zip by topping with chili sauce? And, you know, if you don't have the time, or it's the wrong weather for grilling outdoors, you can use a grill pan to give your burgers a similar look and flavor.

# Bubblin' Beer Dogs

Boy, oh boy, do I remember that restaurant chain that was boiling its hot dogs in beer way back when! How "way" back? Well, let's just say I remember listening to the Four Tops and the Righteous Brothers on the record player during those years. What a tasty memory!

    6 deli-style beef hot dogs (1 pound)
    1 can (12 ounces) beer
    1 cup water
    6 hot dog buns, split

Prick each hot dog several times with a fork. In a large saucepan, bring the beer and water to a boil over high heat. Add the hot dogs and boil for 5 to 6 minutes, until heated through. Serve in the buns with your favorite toppings and maybe even Beefed-Up Chili Sauce (opposite page).

*Did You Know . . .*
July was named National Hot Dog Month
back in 1957?

# Beefed-Up Chili Sauce

This one's gone to the dogs—the hot dogs, that is! And whether we're remembering this hearty taste from years ago or trying it for the first time, it's sure to disappear in a flash.

1 pound lean ground beef
2 cups water
⅓ cup ketchup
1 tablespoon yellow mustard
1 large onion, coarsely chopped
2 tablespoons chili powder
½ teaspoon garlic powder
¼ teaspoon ground red pepper
½ teaspoon salt
⅛ teaspoon black pepper

In a large saucepan, combine all the ingredients and bring to a boil over high heat, stirring until the beef is crumbled. Boil for 20 to 25 minutes, or until most of the liquid is absorbed, stirring occasionally. Serve hot.

*Note:* Perfect as a topping for Bubblin' Beer Dogs (opposite page), but if you prefer to turn this into a traditional chili, just add a 16-ounce can of drained red kidney beans and cook until heated through. Serve in bowls topped with your favorite chili toppings.

# Veggie-Packed Pizza

Years ago, a big night out might have included a date at the local pizzeria, sharing a regular old cheese pizza. These days, things are different. It's not uncommon to stay home and put together a home-made pizza packed with fresh veggies. So why not treat *your* steady?

One 12-inch prepared pizza shell
1 cup pizza sauce (see Note)
1 can (2¼ ounces) sliced black olives, drained
1 jar (2½ ounces) sliced mushrooms, drained
1 jar (7 ounces) roasted red peppers, drained and cut into thin strips
1 cup (4 ounces) shredded mozzarella cheese
1 container (2.8 ounces) French-fried onions

Preheat the oven to 375°F. Place the pizza shell on a pizza pan. Spread with the pizza sauce and top evenly with the black olives, mushrooms, and roasted peppers. Sprinkle with the cheese and French-fried onions. Bake for 15 to 18 minutes, or until the cheese is melted and the crust is crisp and golden. Slice and serve.

*Note:* Use Homemade Pizza Sauce (opposite page) or any ready-made pizza sauce.

# Homemade Pizza Sauce

---
*about 2½ cups*
---

With pizza, the secret's in the sauce. So smother your own creation with this homemade sauce for that flavor of the local pizzeria of yesterday—with the ease of today.

> 1 can (15 ounces) tomato sauce
> 1 can (14½ ounces) diced tomatoes, drained
> 1 garlic clove, minced
> 1 tablespoon dried oregano
> ¼ teaspoon black pepper

In a medium bowl, combine all the ingredients; mix well. Use as a pizza sauce, or heat and serve as a dipping sauce.

**Note:** Place any leftover sauce in an airtight container; it should last that way in the fridge for up to 1 week.

# Stack-'Em-Up Chocolate Chip Pancakes

---

*4 to 6 servings*

---

Remember all those Saturday nights spent at your favorite disco trying to boogie like John Travolta did in *Saturday Night Fever*? Those were the days! And how did you end many of those nights out? By having a big breakfast of chocolate chip pancakes at the local pancake house, I bet! Try this easy recipe for pancakes that look as tempting as the ones on the book's cover.

> 2 cups biscuit baking mix
> 1 cup club soda
> 2 eggs
> 1 teaspoon sugar
> 1 cup (6 ounces) semisweet chocolate chips
> About 2 tablespoons vegetable shortening, divided

In a large bowl, combine the biscuit baking mix, club soda, eggs, and sugar; mix well. Stir in the chocolate chips until well combined. Melt 1 tablespoon vegetable shortening in a nonstick griddle or large skillet over medium heat. Pour ¼ cup batter per pancake onto the griddle and cook the pancakes for about 2 minutes, or until bubbles appear on top. Flip the pancakes and cook for 1 to 2 minutes more, or until golden on both sides, adding more shortening as needed. Serve immediately, or keep warm in a low oven while you cook the remaining pancakes. Serve with Walnut Maple Syrup (opposite page) or your favorite pancake topping.

*Note:* The secret to these light and fluffy pancakes is the club soda—its bubbles add extra air to the batter.

---

# Walnut Maple Syrup

Plain maple syrup is fine, but it's what everybody expects will be served with pancakes. So why not surprise them by creating a fantastic new flavor our pancakes aren't likely to forget. (Neither are we!)

    3 tablespoons butter
    ½ cup chopped walnuts
    1 cup pure maple syrup
    ½ teaspoon vanilla extract

Melt the butter in a small saucepan over medium heat. Add the walnuts and brown for 1 to 2 minutes. Add the maple syrup and vanilla; mix well. Reduce the heat to low and simmer for 2 to 3 minutes, or until heated through, stirring occasionally. Serve warm. Store leftover syrup in a tightly covered container in the refrigerator.

***Note:*** This can be made ahead of time and kept chilled for up to 2 weeks.

# Chart-Toppin' Poultry

Herbed Chicken                          53

Farm-Style Chicken                      54

Garlic Roasted Chicken                  55

The One and Only Fried Chicken          56

Classic Scalloped Chicken               57

American Chicken Chow Mein              58

Chicken à la King                       59

Chicken Potpie                          60

Maple Turkey Sausage                    61

Boastin' Roastin' Turkey Breast         62

Surprise Gravy                          63

# Herbed Chicken

*4 to 6 servings*

This is a great make-ahead dish 'cause you can prepare and bake it one night, then cover it and keep it in the fridge till right before dinner the next night. Just reheat it in a low oven for 20 minutes or so and it'll be ready to make a hit on your dinner table!

½ cup all-purpose flour
½ cup fine dry bread crumbs
1 teaspoon paprika
¼ teaspoon ground thyme
1 teaspoon salt
¼ teaspoon black pepper
One 3- to 4-pound chicken, cut into 8 pieces
¼ cup (½ stick) butter, melted
1 tablespoon vegetable oil

Preheat the oven to 400°F. In a plastic or paper bag, combine the flour, bread crumbs, and seasonings, shaking to mix well. Add 2 or 3 chicken pieces to the bag; shake to coat completely. Remove from the bag and repeat with the remaining chicken. Pour the melted butter and oil into a 9" × 13" baking dish; add the chicken pieces. Bake, uncovered, for 30 minutes. Reduce the oven temperature to 350°F., turn the chicken pieces, and bake for 20 to 25 more minutes, or until cooked through and no pink remains. Serve hot.

# Farm-Style Chicken

This hearty farm-style chicken is sure to satisfy your hungry farmhands—or whoever comes running when the dinner bell rings at your house!

    2 tablespoons olive oil
    One 3- to 3½-pound chicken, cut into 8 pieces
    ¼ teaspoon salt
    ⅛ teaspoon black pepper
    1 large green bell pepper, diced
    1 large onion, diced
    2 garlic cloves, crushed
    1 package (10 ounces) frozen peas

Heat the oil in a large skillet; season the chicken with the salt and pepper and brown on all sides. Remove from the skillet and set aside. Add the green pepper, onion, and garlic to the skillet and cook for about 5 minutes, or until softened, stirring frequently. Return the chicken to the skillet, cover, and cook over medium-low heat for 45 to 50 minutes, stirring often. Gently stir in the frozen peas and cook for another 5 minutes, or until heated through. Serve.

*Note:* I especially like this recipe because it's so versatile, it goes well with potatoes, rice, or noodles.

# Garlic Roasted Chicken

Let's take our favorite roasted chicken and, with the snap of our fingers, add the classic taste of garlic that's as trendy as ever these days!

    One 2½- to 3-pound chicken, cut into 8 pieces
    ¼ cup olive oil
    ½ teaspoon dried oregano
    ½ teaspoon dried basil
    ½ teaspoon salt
    ½ teaspoon black pepper
    1 head garlic, unpeeled, cut crosswise into 3 slices and broken up

Preheat the oven to 350°F. Place the chicken in a 9" × 13" baking dish; set aside. In a small bowl, combine the oil, oregano, basil, salt, and pepper; mix well. Distribute the garlic over the chicken and cover with the oil mixture, drizzling it evenly over the chicken. Bake for 50 to 60 minutes, or until the chicken is golden and no pink remains, turning occasionally. Discard the garlic before serving.

## Did You Know . . .

Before the 1950s, you couldn't hop into your Jacuzzi, make copies using a Xerox machine, or close your sneakers with Velcro— because none of these items had been invented?!

# The One and Only Fried Chicken

There's no substitute for this tried-and-true Southern picnic favorite, so I bet you can't wait to crunch into the taste that's sure never to disappoint! (Check out how crispy and yummy it looks on the cover!)

> One 3- to 3½-pound chicken, cut into 8 pieces
> 3 teaspoons salt, divided
> 1½ cups all-purpose flour
> ¾ teaspoon black pepper
> 2 cups vegetable shortening

Place the chicken in a large bowl and add enough water to cover. Add 2 teaspoons salt and soak for 20 minutes. In a shallow dish, combine the flour, the remaining 1 teaspoon salt, and the pepper; mix well. Remove the chicken from the water and dip in the flour mixture, coating completely. In a large deep skillet, heat the shortening over medium heat until hot but not smoking. Place the coated chicken in the skillet in batches and fry for 8 to 10 minutes per side, or until golden and the juices run clear. Drain on a paper towel—lined platter. Serve immediately.

# Classic Scalloped Chicken

The pages of the calendar seem to get flipped faster and faster every year, but one thing that stays the same is the fact that every day we need to have dinner on the table in a flash—and if it can all be done in one pan, that's a bonus!

- 1½ pounds boneless, skinless chicken breasts, cut into ½-inch chunks
- ½ teaspoon salt
- ¼ teaspoon black pepper
- 4 tablespoons (½ stick) butter, melted, divided
- 1 can (14½ ounces) ready-to-use chicken broth
- 1 jar (12 ounces) chicken gravy
- 1 jar (4½ ounces) sliced mushrooms, drained
- 1 jar (2 ounces) diced pimientos, drained
- 1½ cups instant rice
- ¼ cup plain bread crumbs

Preheat the oven to 400°F. Coat a 9" × 13" baking dish with nonstick cooking spray. Season the chicken with the salt and pepper. Sauté in 2 tablespoons melted butter in a large skillet over medium-high heat for 8 to 10 minutes, or until golden. Remove from the heat and add the chicken broth, chicken gravy, mushrooms, pimientos, and rice; mix well. Pour into the baking dish, cover with aluminum foil, and bake for 30 minutes. Remove from the oven, uncover, and stir well. Sprinkle with the bread crumbs and drizzle with the remaining 2 tablespoons melted butter. Bake uncovered for 5 to 10 minutes, or until the rice is tender and the topping is golden. Serve immediately.

# American Chicken Chow Mein

If we took a trip to the Far East, we'd probably have a hard time finding this one on the menu. Chow mein actually got its start back in Americanized Chinese restaurants after World War II—and once it caught on, there was no stopping it!

    2 tablespoons butter
    1 small onion, finely chopped
    ½ pound fresh mushrooms, sliced
    3 ribs celery, thinly sliced
    1 jar (12 ounces) chicken gravy
    1 can (10 ounces) chunk chicken, drained and flaked
    1 can (14 ounces) bean sprouts, drained
    1 jar (2 ounces) chopped pimientos, drained

Melt the butter in a large skillet over medium heat. Sauté the onion, mushrooms, and celery until tender. Add the remaining ingredients and simmer until heated through, stirring occasionally. Serve immediately.

*Note:* For added crunch, sprinkle with chow mein noodles just before serving.

# Chicken à la King

Don't be fooled by the name. This one's got nothing to do with roy-alty and everything to do with that creamy comfort taste of Mom's cooking that we all remember.

8 tablespoons (1 stick) butter, divided
1½ pounds boneless, skinless chicken breasts, cut into
    ½-inch chunks
6 tablespoons all-purpose flour
1 teaspoon salt
¼ teaspoon black pepper
1 can (14½ ounces) ready-to-use chicken broth
1 cup (½ pint) heavy cream
½ medium green bell pepper, diced
1 jar (2 ounces) chopped pimientos, drained
1 can (4½ ounces) whole mushrooms, drained
2 tablespoons dry sherry (optional)

Melt 2 tablespoons butter in a large skillet over medium-high heat. Sauté the chicken for 5 to 6 minutes, or until no pink remains. Remove the chicken from the skillet; discard the pan juices. Add the remaining 6 tablespoons butter, the flour, salt, and black pepper to the skillet and cook, whisking constantly, until the butter melts. Slowly add the chicken broth and cream and bring to a boil, whisk-ing until smooth and thickened. Reduce the heat to medium-low, return the chicken to the skillet, and add the remaining ingredients. Simmer until heated through, stirring constantly. Serve immediately.

# Chicken Potpie

---

*6 servings*

---

Just like we remember watching variety shows of the 1960s and '70s, we think back to the basic comfort tastes of Mom's made-from-scratch dinners, too . . . and we miss them! Wanna bring 'em back again? We can do it faster than we can say, "I want my MTV!"

    2 tablespoons butter
    1 pound boneless, skinless chicken breasts,
        cut into ½-inch chunks
    ¾ teaspoon salt
    ½ teaspoon black pepper
    1 package (16 ounces) frozen peas and carrots
    1 can (14½ ounces) whole potatoes, drained and coarsely chopped
    1 jar (12 ounces) chicken gravy
    1 package (15 ounces) folded refrigerated pie crusts

Preheat the oven to 400°F. Melt the butter in a large skillet over medium-high heat. Season the chicken with the salt and pepper and sauté for 4 to 6 minutes, or until no pink remains. Add the peas and carrots, potatoes, and gravy; mix well and remove from the heat. Unfold 1 pie crust and place it in a 9-inch deep-dish pie plate, pressing the crust firmly into the plate. Spoon the chicken mixture into the crust. Unfold the second pie crust and place it over the chicken mixture. Pinch together and trim the edges to seal, then flute, if desired. Using a sharp knife, cut four 1-inch slits in the top. Bake for 40 to 45 minutes, or until the filling is heated through and the crust is golden. Allow to sit for 10 minutes before serving.

# Maple Turkey Sausage

These days we're all watching our waistlines, so many of us avoid serving the sausage we grew up seeing regularly on the breakfast table. Here's a simple solution: homemade breakfast sausage that uses ground turkey. Same super flavor, but definitely on the lighter side!

1 pound ground turkey breast (see Note)
1 small onion, finely chopped
1 egg
3 tablespoons maple syrup
2 tablespoons plain dry bread crumbs
1 teaspoon dried thyme
1 teaspoon fennel seeds
½ teaspoon rubbed sage
½ teaspoon salt
¼ teaspoon ground red pepper
¼ teaspoon black pepper

In a large bowl, combine all the ingredients; mix well. Form the mixture into sixteen 3-inch-long sausage links. Coat a large skillet with nonstick cooking spray. Heat the skillet over medium heat. Add the sausage; cover and cook for 6 to 8 minutes, or until no pink remains, turning to brown completely. Serve immediately.

**Note:** Using ground turkey *breast*—not just ground turkey—assures you that you are getting the leanest type of ground turkey.

# Boastin' Roastin' Turkey Breast

*6 servings*

Roasted turkey—mmm, mmm, it's comfort food we can all enjoy. Sure, when we buy it premade, it's an option that helps us get dinner on the table fast. But now it's time to get ready for a meal that you can boast about . . . 'cause not only does it taste great, but you've made it yourself!

> 3 tablespoons butter, melted
> 1 teaspoon garlic salt
> ½ teaspoon rubbed sage
> ¼ teaspoon black pepper
> One 5-pound turkey breast

Preheat the oven to 375°F. In a small bowl, combine the butter, garlic salt, sage, and pepper; mix well. Place the turkey breast in a roasting pan and brush with the seasoning mixture. Cover with aluminum foil and bake for 50 minutes. Uncover and bake for 40 to 45 minutes more, or until no pink remains and the juices run clear, basting occasionally. Remove from the oven and allow to sit for 15 to 20 minutes, then slice and serve with Surprise Gravy (opposite page).

***Note:*** Turkey is available already cut into parts either fresh or frozen at your local supermarket. If you are buying it frozen, make sure to allow time for it to thaw in the refrigerator before roasting.

# Surprise Gravy

Wanna know the surprise? The cranberries *and* the gravy are both here, making this a two-in-one bonus that's oh-so-tasty.

    1 jar (12 ounces) turkey gravy
    2 tablespoons sweetened dried cranberries (see Note)
    1 tablespoon white wine

In a small saucepan, combine all the ingredients over medium-low heat. Simmer for 6 to 8 minutes, or until heated through, stirring occasionally. Serve immediately.

***Note:*** Sweetened dried cranberries are usually available in the supermarket in the dried fruit section, near the raisins.

# Outta-Sight Meats

TV Dinner Meat Loaf — 67

Mom's Pot Roast — 68

Family Spaghetti and Meatballs — 69

Simmerin' Swiss Steak — 70

Stew-pendous Goulash — 71

Diner-Style Liver and Onions — 72

Apple Pork Chops — 73

Tangy Roasted Spareribs — 74

Roast Pork in a Bag — 75

Pineapple Baked Ham — 76

Lamb Kebabs — 77

Veal Birds — 78

# TV Dinner Meat Loaf

*4 to 6 servings*

Not long after television first came into our living rooms, food became a big part of the TV-watching experience. We'd plop down on the couch in front of the screen and dig into something new we'd found in the market—frozen TV dinners. The first ones were simple home-style menus, featuring main courses like roast turkey and meat loaf. Why not try this homemade version that reminds us of those first dinners we enjoyed in front of the TV?

1½ pounds ground beef
3 slices white bread, torn into small pieces
1 small onion, finely chopped
1 egg
¼ cup milk
¼ teaspoon dry mustard
1 teaspoon salt
¼ teaspoon black pepper
3 tablespoons ketchup

Preheat the oven to 350°F. In a large bowl, combine all the ingredients except the ketchup; mix well. Press the mixture evenly into a 9" × 5" loaf pan. Spread the ketchup over the top and bake for 60 to 65 minutes, or until no pink remains and the juices run clear. Remove from the oven; drain and allow to sit for 5 minutes. Slice and serve.

***Note:*** If you prefer to pass on the ketchup, that's okay; you could use spaghetti sauce or just leave it plain.

# Mom's Pot Roast

## 4 to 6 servings

Think about it—the Cleavers, the Cunninghams, the Bradys—the sit-com families we grew up with always sat down to dinner . . . *together!* These days, a sit-down family dinner seems old-fashioned. Well, let me tell you, it's the best thing we can do for our families, so let's go back in time and make a meal that we can all enjoy the way they did.

> ½ cup all-purpose flour
> 2 teaspoons salt
> ½ teaspoon black pepper
> One 4-pound boneless beef chuck roast
> ¼ cup vegetable oil
> 4 cups water
> ½ cup prepared white horseradish
> 4 medium potatoes, peeled and quartered
> 4 medium carrots, cut into 1-inch chunks
> 2 medium onions, cut into wedges

In a large bowl, combine the flour, salt, and pepper; mix well. Rinse the roast and, while it's still wet, add to the flour mixture, coating completely. Heat the oil in a soup pot over medium-high heat. Add the beef and cook for 10 to 12 minutes, turning to brown on all sides. Add the water and horseradish and bring to a boil. Reduce the heat to medium-low, cover loosely, and simmer for 1½ hours. Add the remaining ingredients; cover loosely and simmer for 40 to 45 minutes, or until the meat and vegetables are fork-tender. Remove the roast to a cutting board. Slice and serve with the vegetables and sauce.

# Family Spaghetti and Meatballs

We often turn back the hands of time to seek out the origin of recipes our families have enjoyed for years and years. Spaghetti and meatballs is one of them. Everybody's family makes it just a little differently. Of course, all our modern conveniences make any recipe easier—but this one also has the wholesome tastes we've loved for so long.

> 1 pound ground beef
> 1 egg
> ½ small green bell pepper, finely chopped
> 2 tablespoons grated Parmesan cheese
> 1 teaspoon dried oregano
> 1 teaspoon salt
> ½ small onion, chopped
> 1 jar (26 ounces) spaghetti sauce
> 1 pound spaghetti

In a large bowl, combine the ground beef, egg, pepper, Parmesan cheese, oregano, and salt. Mix well and form into 12 meatballs. In a soup pot, brown the meatballs with the onion over medium-high heat for 8 to 10 minutes. Add the spaghetti sauce; bring to a boil. Reduce the heat to medium-low and simmer for 35 to 40 minutes, or until no pink remains in the beef, stirring occasionally. Meanwhile, prepare the spaghetti according to the package directions; drain. Serve the meatballs and sauce over the spaghetti.

*Note:* Go ahead and add some garlic or any other favorite seasonings to the sauce, if you want, or, if you have time, make your own sauce from scratch. It's *your* family dish.

# Simmerin' Swiss Steak

With today's busy lifestyles, we're always looking for quick solutions. Whether it's a speed-dial button on the phone, quick-drying nail polish, or instant foods, we want everything fast and we want it now. Or even yesterday! Although we all enjoy those easy shortcuts of today, every once in a while it's nice not to rush. So why not surprise the family with a meal made from scratch, like our moms used to make?

1½ pounds beef cubed steaks
½ teaspoon salt
½ teaspoon black pepper
½ cup all-purpose flour
3 tablespoons vegetable oil
1 medium onion, chopped
1 can (28 ounces) Italian-style diced tomatoes, undrained

Season the cube steaks with the salt and pepper. Dip the steaks in the flour, coating completely. Heat the oil in a large skillet over medium-high heat. Add half of the steaks and cook for 2 to 3 minutes per side, or until browned. Remove the steaks to a platter and cook the remaining steaks. Return all the steaks to the skillet and add the remaining ingredients. Cook over low heat for 18 to 20 minutes, or until the sauce is thickened and the meat is tender, stirring occasionally. Serve the steaks topped with the sauce from the pan.

***Note:*** Serve with Special Spaetzle (page 118) or just boil up a batch of ready-made wide noodles.

# Stew-pendous Goulash

When we want to recapture the home-cooked aromas and tastes of our childhood, a hearty stew or goulash is just what we need. This one goes together quickly, but it cooks long enough to satisfy our taste buds—and all the rest of our senses, too!

    ¼ cup (½ stick) butter
    1½ pounds beef round steak, cut into 1-inch chunks
    2 large onions, quartered
    2 medium potatoes, peeled and quartered
    4 carrots, cut into 1-inch chunks
    2 cups water
    1 can (14½ ounces) ready-to-use beef broth
    1 teaspoon paprika
    ½ teaspoon black pepper
    2 medium tomatoes, chopped

Melt the butter in a soup pot over high heat. Add the steak, onions, potatoes, and carrots and cook for 12 to 15 minutes, or until browned, stirring frequently. Add the water, broth, paprika, and pepper and bring to a boil. Reduce the heat to medium, cover, and simmer for 1 hour. Add the tomatoes and simmer uncovered for 30 to 40 minutes, or until the beef is tender and the sauce is thickened.

***Note:*** Serve this over medium egg noodles so you don't miss any of the sauce.

# Diner-Style Liver and Onions

Calling all liver lovers! This diner classic is just for you. And if you've never tried it, there's no need to head out to the local diner, 'cause you can make this so easily right at home.

> ¼ pound sliced bacon (see Note)
> 2 large onions, thinly sliced
> 2 tablespoons all-purpose flour
> ½ teaspoon salt
> ¼ teaspoon black pepper
> 1½ pounds beef liver, sliced into steaks

In a large skillet, cook the bacon over medium heat until crisp. Remove the bacon from the skillet and set aside, leaving the drippings in the skillet. Add the onions to the skillet and sauté over medium-high heat until caramelized. Remove to a bowl and cover to keep warm. In a shallow dish, combine the flour, salt, and pepper; mix well. Coat the liver lightly with the flour mixture, add to the skillet, and cook over medium-high heat for 4 to 5 minutes per side, or until brown and cooked through. Remove the liver to a platter then top with the onions. Crumble the bacon and sprinkle over the onions.

***Note:*** If you prefer to leave out the bacon, caramelize the onions in 2 tablespoons vegetable oil.

# Apple Pork Chops

These are a twist on the combo of pork chops and applesauce—a classic if there ever was one!

½ cup all-purpose flour
1 teaspoon salt
½ teaspoon black pepper
6 pork loin chops (about 3 pounds total), 1 inch thick (see Note)
¼ cup vegetable oil
1 container (21 ounces) apple pie filling
½ cup water

In a shallow dish, combine the flour, salt, and pepper; mix well. Dip the pork chops in the flour mixture, coating completely. In a large deep skillet, heat the oil over medium-high heat. Add the chops and brown for 4 to 5 minutes per side. Stir in the pie filling and water. Cook for 3 to 4 minutes, or until no pink remains in the chops. Serve with the sauce spooned over the top.

*Note:* To get nice thick pork chops, ask your butcher or the meat cutter at the grocery store to cut them fresh for you.

# Tangy Roasted Spareribs

*4 to 6 servings*

We've all enjoyed a juicy hot dog smothered in sauerkraut, right? Why not take that one step further and combine savory sauerkraut with spareribs for a taste that blends the best of yesterday and today?

  1 package (2 pounds) sauerkraut, rinsed and drained
  1 teaspoon caraway seeds
  2 racks pork spareribs (about 3 pounds each)
  2 envelopes (1 ounce each) onion soup mix
  2 medium onions, thinly sliced
  ½ teaspoon black pepper

Preheat the oven to 350°F. Coat two 9" × 13" baking dishes with non-stick cooking spray. In a medium bowl, combine the sauerkraut and caraway seeds; mix well and spread equally in the two baking dishes. Place a rack of ribs over the sauerkraut in each dish. Sprinkle evenly with the onion soup mix, top with the onions, and sprinkle with the pepper. Cover with aluminum foil and bake for 1¼ hours. Uncover and bake for 20 to 30 minutes more, or until the ribs are tender. Cut into individual ribs and serve with the sauerkraut.

## Did You Know . . .

In the 1950s, Dick Clark's *American Bandstand,* the music/dance show geared to teens—and the granddaddy of MTV—was one of the most-watched daytime TV shows, with an average audience of 8.5 million?

# Roast Pork in a Bag

## 6 servings

Some of us might think that oven bags are a modern invention, but foil cooking goes back a long time. It's a simple way to capture lots of juicy flavor and cook it into our food.

One 2½-pound boneless pork loin roast
⅔ cup packed light brown sugar
¼ cup applesauce
1½ teaspoons ground ginger
1 teaspoon cornstarch
2 teaspoons water

1 oven bag (see Note)

Preheat the oven to 325°F. Place the roast in the oven bag, then place the bag in a 9" × 13" baking dish. In a small bowl, combine the brown sugar, applesauce, and ginger; mix well. Spoon over the roast; seal the bag, then cut six 1-inch slits in the top. Bake for 55 to 60 minutes, or until little pink remains for medium-well, or no pink remains for well-done. In a small bowl, combine the cornstarch and water; mix well. In a medium saucepan, combine the pan drippings from the bag and the cornstarch mixture. Cook over high heat for 2 to 3 minutes, or until the sauce begins to thicken, stirring constantly. Cut the roast into thin slices and serve with the gravy spooned over the top.

*Note:* Oven bags can be found in the paper goods/food wraps area of the supermarket, near the aluminum foil and plastic wrap.

# Pineapple Baked Ham

Once upon a time, canned hams were big . . . really big. They were sautéed, baked, fried, and prepared just about any way we can imagine. And yes, we even ate fruit glazes way back then, too. Those are more popular than ever, so give this fruity dish a try!

One 3-pound canned ham
1 package (4-serving size) pineapple-flavored gelatin
½ cup packed light brown sugar
2 teaspoons water

Preheat the oven to 350°F. Coat a 9" × 13" baking dish with nonstick cooking spray. Place the ham in the baking dish. In a small bowl, combine the gelatin mix, brown sugar, and water; mix well until a paste forms and spread over the top of the ham. Bake for 1 hour, or until heated through, basting occasionally with the pan juices. Slice and serve.

***Note:*** It's easy to make a nice sauce to serve along with the ham—just heat some pineapple preserves in a small saucepan until melted.

# Lamb Kebabs

Back in the '50s, lamb kebabs were really popular, but virtually anything that could be threaded onto a skewer was barbecued or broiled, since a kebab meal was easy to prepare and fun to serve . . . and still is!

1 bottle (8 ounces) Italian dressing
½ small onion, finely chopped
3 garlic cloves, minced
1 tablespoon chili powder
1 tablespoon curry powder
¼ teaspoon salt
24 pitted ripe olives
4 large bell peppers (2 each red and green), each cut into 18 chunks
1½ pounds boneless leg of lamb, cut into thirty-six 1-inch chunks
1 medium eggplant, cut into 36 cubes
Twelve 12-inch wooden skewers

In a small bowl, make a marinade by combining the Italian dressing, onion, garlic, chili powder, curry powder, and salt; mix well and set aside. Alternately skewer 2 olives and 3 pieces each of red pepper, green pepper, lamb, and eggplant on each skewer. Brush the kebabs with the marinade and place in a 9" × 13" baking dish. Pour any remaining marinade over the kebabs; cover and marinate in the refrigerator for at least 4 hours, or overnight, turning occasionally. Preheat the broiler. Coat two large rimmed baking sheets with nonstick cooking spray. Place the kebabs on the baking sheets and drizzle with the marinade from the baking dish. Broil for 5 to 6 minutes per side, or until the lamb is cooked to medium, or to desired doneness beyond that. Serve immediately.

# Veal Birds

## 6 servings

At one time, this elegant stuffed and rolled dish was really popular in fancy restaurants. Why not try my easy version that's sure to fly right off your table?

> 6 veal cutlets (about 1½ pounds total), pounded to ¼-inch thickness
> ½ teaspoon black pepper, divided
> 6 thin slices (about ⅓ pound) deli ham
> 1 cup (4 ounces) shredded mozzarella cheese
> 1 cup plain bread crumbs
> 1 egg
> ½ cup plus 2 tablespoons milk, divided
> 1 can (10¾ ounces) reduced-sodium condensed cream of mushroom soup
> ½ teaspoon seasoning and browning sauce

Preheat the oven to 350°F. Coat a 9" × 13" baking dish with nonstick cooking spray. Season the cutlets with ¼ teaspoon pepper. Top each piece with a slice of ham and a sprinkle of cheese; roll up jelly-roll style. Place the bread crumbs in a shallow dish. In another shallow dish, combine the egg and 2 tablespoons milk; mix well. Dip each veal roll in the egg mixture, then the bread crumbs, coating completely; place in the baking dish. In a small bowl, combine the soup, seasoning and browning sauce, and the remaining ½ cup milk and ¼ teaspoon pepper; mix well and spoon over the veal rolls. Cover with aluminum foil and bake for 1 hour. Uncover and bake for 8 to 10 minutes more, or until the sauce is thickened. Serve the veal birds topped with the sauce.

*Note:* The type of ham used will determine how salty this dish is.

# Far-out Fish and Seafood

Buttermilk-Fried Fish                      81

Our Own Fish Sticks                        82

Fast Tartar Sauce                          83

Classic Tuna Noodle Bake                   84

Shortcut Lobster Newburg                   85

Macadamia-Crusted Mahimahi                 86

Salmon Croquettes                          87

Not-Stuffed "Stuffed" Salmon               88

Perfect Fried Shrimp                       89

# Buttermilk-Fried Fish

Don't shy away from buttermilk. It adds a rich taste of the past.

> 2 pounds white-fleshed fish fillets, such as cod, perch, or
>     haddock, thawed if frozen
> 1 cup buttermilk
> 1 cup biscuit baking mix
> 1 teaspoon salt
> Vegetable oil for panfrying

Cut the fish into serving-sized portions and place in a shallow dish. Pour the buttermilk over the fish, cover, and refrigerate for 30 minutes, turning once. In a large bowl, combine the biscuit mix and salt; remove the fish from the buttermilk and coat with the biscuit mix mixture. Heat ¼ inch oil in a large skillet; place the fish in the skillet in a single layer and cook until the fish flakes easily with a fork, turning to brown on both sides. Drain on paper towels and serve.

## Did You Know . . .
The average price of a new car in 1955 was $1,910?

# Our Own Fish Sticks

When these first appeared in the mid-'50s in the grocer's freezer case, they created quite a stir. Today, if we're fishing for a more homemade taste, we can custom-make our own easily!

2 eggs
3 tablespoons sour cream
1½ cups Italian-flavored bread crumbs
1½ pounds frozen white-fleshed fish fillets, thawed and
    cut into 1" × 4" strips
¼ teaspoon salt
¼ teaspoon black pepper
½ cup vegetable oil

In a small bowl, combine the eggs and sour cream; mix well. Place the bread crumbs in a shallow dish. Season the fish with the salt and pepper. Dip each fish strip into the egg mixture, then the bread crumbs, coating completely. Heat the oil in a large skillet over medium-high heat. Add the fish strips and cook for 6 to 8 minutes, or until the fish flakes easily with a fork, turning to brown all sides. Serve immediately as is or with Fast Tartar Sauce (opposite page).

***Note:*** Sometimes it's easier to cut the fish into strips while it's slightly frozen, then thaw completely before continuing. And you wanna know the secret to coating the fish strips just right? Use one hand to dip the fish into the egg mixture and the other hand to coat the fish with the bread crumbs. Keeping one hand dry will keep the bread crumbs from getting all clumped together.

# Fast Tartar Sauce

Sure, it's easy to open a jar—but if we really wanna show we care, this one mixes up in minutes. And you just can't beat that fresh "I made it myself" taste of yesterday!

 1 cup mayonnaise
 ¼ cup sweet pickle relish
 2 scallions, finely chopped
 1 tablespoon capers
 ⅛ teaspoon ground red pepper

In a small bowl, combine all the ingredients; mix well. Serve, or cover and chill until ready to use.

**Note:** This will hold well in a tightly sealed jar in the refrigerator for several weeks.

# Classic Tuna Noodle Bake

Even if we aren't kids anymore, certain things still make us smile and feel good—like the foods of our childhood . . . especially tuna noodle casserole. It's a classic.

  1 package (8 ounces) medium egg noodles
  1 can (10¾ ounces) condensed cream of mushroom soup
  1 cup milk
  1 can (12 ounces) chunk tuna, drained and flaked
  1 jar (2 ounces) diced pimientos, drained
  ⅛ teaspoon black pepper
  1 cup crushed potato chips

Preheat the oven to 350°F. Prepare the noodles according to the package directions; drain. Coat a 9" × 13" baking dish with nonstick cooking spray. In a large bowl, combine the soup and milk; mix well. Add the noodles, tuna, pimientos, and pepper; mix well. Pour into the baking dish and top evenly with the potato chips. Bake for 30 to 35 minutes, or until bubbly and heated through. Serve immediately.

***Note:*** If you want to make this in advance, just put it together and keep it chilled until ready to top with the crushed potato chips and bake.

# Shortcut Lobster Newburg

If you want to remember the tastes of a big Saturday night out, here's a shortcut to the fancy flavors of the past.

1 pound imitation crabmeat, cut into 1-inch chunks
2 cans (15 ounces each) lobster bisque
¼ cup dry sherry

In a large saucepan, combine all the ingredients and cook over medium heat until heated through, stirring occasionally. Serve.

*Note:* For a really elegant main dish, serve this over Speedy Almond Rice (page 124) or any of your favorite rice dishes.

# Macadamia-Crusted Mahimahi

In the 1950s, when the Hawaiian rage was in full swing, Trader Vic's restaurants were popping up to serve all sorts of traditional South Pacific favorites. This simple dish is winning loads of new fans today. And if you've never tried macadamia nuts, boy, are you in for a treat!

> One 2-pound fresh mahimahi fillet, cut into 6 pieces
> Juice of 1 lemon
> ½ teaspoon salt
> ¼ teaspoon black pepper
> 1 cup chopped macadamia nuts (see Note)
> 2 tablespoons butter, melted

Preheat the oven to 350°F. Place the mahimahi fillets on a rimmed baking sheet. Season with the lemon juice, salt, and pepper. Top with the macadamia nuts and drizzle with the melted butter. Bake for 20 to 22 minutes, or until the fish flakes easily with a fork. Serve immediately.

**Note:** Instead of using a chopper to chop the nuts, place them on a cutting board and use a knife to cut them into equal-sized pieces—that way they won't get too finely chopped.

# Salmon Croquettes

This is one of my family's favorite recipes that keeps getting updated with the times.

> 2 cans (14¾ ounces each) pink or red salmon, drained,
>     boned, and flaked
> 4 eggs, beaten
> ⅔ cup instant mashed potato flakes
> 2 tablespoons finely chopped fresh parsley
> ½ small onion, finely chopped
> ¼ teaspoon salt
> ½ teaspoon black pepper
> ¼ cup plain bread crumbs
> About 4 tablespoons (½ stick) butter

In a large bowl, combine all the ingredients except the bread crumbs and butter; mix well. Shape into twelve ½-inch-thick round patties. Place the bread crumbs in a shallow dish. Coat each patty completely with the bread crumbs. In a large skillet, heat 2 tablespoons butter over medium heat. Cook the patties in batches for 4 to 5 minutes per side, or until golden brown, adding more butter as needed. Serve immediately, or rewarm in a low oven just before serving.

***Note:*** My favorite way to enjoy these is to serve them with an easy dill sauce made by combining 1 cup sour cream, ½ cup mayonnaise, 1 tablespoon sweet pickle relish, 2 teaspoons lemon juice, and 1 teaspoon dried dillweed until well mixed. It can be made ahead and chilled until ready to serve.

# Not-Stuffed "Stuffed" Salmon

*6 servings*

Traditionally, whole fish was always served stuffed, and that's quite a job! Well, I've simplified things by placing the stuffing over a fillet. We get the same tasty result with lots less work!

One 2-pound salmon fillet
½ teaspoon salt
¼ teaspoon black pepper
1 package (8 ounces) corn bread stuffing, prepared according to
    the package directions
¼ cup (½ stick) butter, melted

Preheat the oven to 425°F. Coat a 9" × 13" baking dish with nonstick cooking spray. Season the salmon with the salt and pepper; place in the baking dish. Cover the salmon with the prepared stuffing and drizzle with the butter. Bake for 35 to 40 minutes, or until the fish flakes easily with a fork. Serve whole on a platter, or cut into individual portions to serve.

# Perfect Fried Shrimp

Packaged fried shrimp may be available in most supermarket freezer sections these days, but sometimes you just want the classic made-from-scratch version.

> ¾ cup all-purpose flour
> 1 tablespoon baking powder
> 1 teaspoon salt
> 1 teaspoon ground red pepper
> 2 eggs
> ¼ cup milk
> ½ cup vegetable oil
> 1½ pounds large shrimp, peeled and deveined, tails left on

In a shallow dish, combine the flour, baking powder, salt, and ground red pepper; mix well. In another shallow dish, beat the eggs and milk with a fork until well combined. In a large skillet, heat the oil over medium-high heat until hot but not smoking. Dip the shrimp in the flour mixture, then in the egg mixture, and then again in the flour mixture, coating completely. Cook the shrimp for about 1 minute per side, or until the coating is golden and the shrimp are cooked through. Drain on a paper towel–lined platter. Serve immediately.

***Note:*** Cocktail sauce, tartar sauce (like the one on page 83) or any of your favorite dipping sauces can be served with these shrimp.

# Groovy Vegetables

Lemon-Chive Asparagus　93

Backyard Bean Bake　94

Pearlized Green Beans　95

Tangy Harvard Beets　96

Broccoli with Mock Hollandaise　97

Saucy Brussels Sprouts　98

Glazed Baby Carrots　99

Sweet Peas and Carrots　100

Light 'n' Cheesy Cauliflower　101

Spicy Lime Corn on the Cob　102

Special Creamed Spinach　103

Parmesan-Baked Tomatoes　104

Zucchini and Tomato Bake　105

Vegetable Cornucopia　106

# Lemon-Chive Asparagus

*4 to 6 servings*

Remember those old-fashioned juicers? You'd squeeze and squeeze with all your might and, if you were lucky, maybe you'd get a spoonful or two of juice. Now we've got electric juicers, so with an easy squeeze we've got fresh lemon juice—a super addition to dressings and marinades, and a zippy topping for steamed veggies.

 1 cup water
 ½ teaspoon salt
 1½ pounds fresh asparagus, trimmed
 ¼ cup (½ stick) butter
 1 teaspoon grated lemon peel
 2 tablespoons fresh lemon juice
 1 tablespoon minced fresh chives (see Note)

Bring the water and salt to a boil in a large skillet over high heat. Add the asparagus; reduce the heat to low, cover, and simmer for 8 to 10 minutes, or until the asparagus is tender. Drain and arrange on a serving platter. In the same skillet, melt the butter over medium-high heat. Stir in the remaining ingredients; mix well, then pour over the asparagus. Serve immediately.

*Note:* I like to garnish the platter with slices of fresh lemon. Oh—if you don't have fresh chives, 1 teaspoon of freeze-dried chives can be substituted for 1 tablespoon of minced fresh.

# Backyard Bean Bake

Backyard barbecues were big in the '50s, as more and more young couples moved to the "burbs"—you know, the suburbs. Back then, built-in brick barbecues were all the rage, with the backyard being the new frontier for exploring undiscovered recipes like these tangy baked beans.

> 2 cans (16 ounces each) baked beans
> 2 cans (2.8 ounces each) French-fried onions
> ¼ cup molasses
> 3 tablespoons real bacon bits
> 2 tablespoons yellow mustard
> 1 tablespoon butter, softened

Preheat the oven to 350°F. Coat an 8-inch square baking dish with nonstick cooking spray. In a medium bowl, combine all the ingredients except 1 can of the French-fried onions; mix well and pour into the baking dish. Top with the remaining can of French-fried onions and bake for 25 to 30 minutes, or until bubbly and the onions are golden. Serve immediately.

***Note:*** These can also be made on a barbecue grill. Just prepare them in a disposable aluminum pan that you can place right on the grill rack to cook until heated through.

# Pearlized Green Beans

What happens if we match fresh green beans with cute-as-can-be frozen pearl onions? We get a side dish that says "fresh from the garden with half the work"!

    1 pound fresh green beans, trimmed
    1 package (16 ounces) frozen pearl onions, thawed
    ¼ cup (½ stick) butter, melted
    ½ teaspoon dried basil
    ½ teaspoon garlic powder
    1 teaspoon salt
    ½ teaspoon black pepper

Place the green beans in a large saucepan and add enough water to cover them. Bring to a boil over high heat and cook for 8 minutes. Add the onions and cook for 5 to 7 minutes, or until tender; drain. Add the remaining ingredients; mix well and serve.

***Note:*** Fresh green beans are now available already cleaned, trimmed, and ready for use in the produce department of many supermarkets; or, if you prefer, you can thaw and use a 16-ounce package of frozen green beans.

# Tangy Harvard Beets

It sure doesn't matter what the calendar says the year is, it's always been a challenge getting kids to eat right. Maybe this colorful side dish will catch their eyes and win over their taste buds.

> 2 tablespoons butter
> 2 tablespoons all-purpose flour
> 2 cans (15 ounces each) whole baby beets, drained, with the liquid reserved from 1 can, and quartered
> 2 tablespoons apple cider vinegar
> 1 teaspoon sugar

Melt the butter in a medium saucepan over medium heat. Add the flour and whisk until smooth. Add the reserved beet liquid, the cider vinegar, and sugar, and cook, whisking, until the mixture is thickened and reduced by half. Add the beets and cook until heated through and glazed. Serve immediately.

**Note:** To give these a bit more tang, use an additional 1 to 2 tablespoons of apple cider vinegar.

# Broccoli with Mock Hollandaise

"Mock" was "in" in the '50s and '60s. Everybody was trying new ways of simplifying fancy-sounding recipes. And today, with how busy we all are, it's a better idea than ever!

2 packages (10 ounces each) frozen broccoli spears
4 ounces cream cheese
1 egg
2 tablespoons fresh lemon juice
¼ teaspoon salt
¼ teaspoon black pepper

Cook the broccoli spears according to the package directions; drain if necessary. Meanwhile, in a small saucepan, combine the remaining ingredients over low heat; mix well. Cook for 2 to 3 minutes, or until the sauce is smooth and thick, stirring constantly. Serve over the broccoli spears.

**Note:** If you want to use fresh broccoli, just cut a bunch into spears and steam until tender.

# Saucy Brussels Sprouts

For years, béarnaise sauce has been a popular accompaniment to steaks. Now, by adding some to our brussels sprouts, we get a prime-tasting side dish.

  2 packages (10 ounces each) frozen brussels sprouts (see Note)
  ¼ cup (½ stick) butter
  1 package (⅞ ounce) béarnaise sauce mix
  1 cup milk
  1 teaspoon yellow mustard

Cook the brussels sprouts according to the package directions; drain. Melt the butter in a medium skillet over medium heat. Add the béarnaise sauce mix; mix well. Add the milk and mustard and bring to a boil. Cook for 1 minute, or until thickened, stirring constantly. Add the brussels sprouts and stir until well coated and heated through. Serve immediately.

*Note:* If using fresh brussels sprouts, trim the stems and peel off the tough outer leaves, if necessary, then boil the trimmed brussels sprouts in salted water until tender before proceeding as directed above.

# Glazed Baby Carrots

In the early days of TV, sitcom moms spent all day cooking hearty meals in their best dresses and pearls. Well, the head of the kitchen today may be in a business suit or a jogging suit—in fact, it may not even be mom! A lot of dads and kids have gotten into the act, too. And even though they may not have as much time on their hands as those TV moms, they've got super-easy recipes to help them turn out plenty of main-dish and side-dish winners—like this one—that bring real satisfaction.

¼ cup (½ stick) butter
2 tablespoons apple jelly
2 cans (14½ ounces each) baby carrots, drained (see Note)

Melt the butter and apple jelly in a medium saucepan over medium heat, stirring occasionally. Add the carrots and cook for 5 to 6 minutes, or until heated through, stirring frequently. Serve.

**Note:** Fresh baby carrots can also be used, but they need to be boiled or steamed until tender before proceeding as directed above.

# Sweet Peas and Carrots

From turkey and mashed potatoes to penne with roasted vegetables and tomatoes, today's TV dinners offer us more choices than ever. These days, there's certainly something for everybody, from hearty dinners "like mom used to make" to light meals and everything in between! And the side dishes—why, they're tastier than ever, just like these sweet, crunchy peas and carrots that we can easily make ourselves.

   ¼ cup (½ stick) butter
   1 package (16 ounces) frozen whole baby carrots,
      thawed (see Note)
   1 package (16 ounces) frozen sugar snap peas,
      thawed (see Note)
   1 can (8 ounces) sliced water chestnuts, drained
   3 tablespoons honey
   ½ teaspoon salt

Melt the butter in a large skillet over medium-high heat. Sauté the carrots for 6 minutes. Stir in the remaining ingredients and sauté for 2 to 3 minutes, or until heated through. Serve immediately.

*Note:* Fresh baby carrots and sugar snap peas can be used as long as you boil them until tender first, then proceed as above.

# Light 'n' Cheesy Cauliflower

Love cheesy vegetable dishes but wish they were lighter? Here you go! One taste and you're gonna be asking, "How can something this yummy and cheesy be lighter, too?!"

4 cups water
1 teaspoon salt
1 large head cauliflower, trimmed and cut into florets
1 cup (4 ounces) shredded reduced-fat sharp Cheddar cheese
½ cup light mayonnaise
2 teaspoons yellow mustard
⅛ teaspoon black pepper

In a large saucepan, bring the water and salt to a boil over medium-high heat. Add the cauliflower. Reduce the heat to low, cover, and cook for 10 minutes, or until tender; drain in a colander and set aside.
In the same saucepan, combine the remaining ingredients. Cook over low heat for 3 to 5 minutes, or until the cheese is melted, stirring frequently. Add the cauliflower and stir gently until heated through. Serve immediately.

***Note:*** If you prefer, place the cooked cauliflower in a baking dish and top with the cheese sauce. Bake at 350°F. for 15 to 20 minutes, or until golden. Serve immediately, or prepare ahead of time and keep chilled until ready to bake and serve.

# Spicy Lime Corn on the Cob

*6 servings*

Corn on the cob was and still is a must-have at a cookout. And one taste of this tangy lime-buttered corn will explain why the '50s fad of foil cooking is still with us!

   ¼ cup (½ stick) butter, melted
   Juice of 1 lime
   ½ teaspoon ground red pepper
   ¼ teaspoon salt
   6 ears fresh corn, husked

Preheat the grill to medium heat. In a small bowl, combine all the ingredients except the corn; mix well. Place each ear of corn on a piece of aluminum foil; brush with the butter mixture and wrap tightly in the aluminum foil. Grill for 18 to 22 minutes, or until tender. Carefully unwrap the corn and serve.

***Note:*** To lighten this up, just replace the butter with a bit of fat-free Italian dressing for guilt-free flavored corn on the cob.

# Special Creamed Spinach

## 4 to 6 servings

Turn on the radio these days and you hear lots of remakes of classic songs—many with updated beats. In fact, in dance clubs around the country, today's young people are swinging to the music of the '40s and twirling to '70s disco music! That trend has spread to our dinner tables, too, 'cause old favorites like creamed spinach are showing up and winning a whole new generation of fans.

    3 tablespoons butter
    1 garlic clove, minced
    3 tablespoons all-purpose flour
    1 teaspoon salt
    2 cups (1 pint) half-and-half
    2 packages (9 ounces each) frozen chopped spinach,
        thawed and squeezed dry

Melt the butter in a medium saucepan over medium heat. Add the garlic and cook until soft. Add the flour and salt and whisk until smooth. Slowly pour in the half-and-half, whisking until smooth and thickened. Add the spinach; mix well and cook until heated through. Serve immediately.

### Did You Know . . .

Before the grooved 12-inch LP record was invented in the 1950s, music was recorded on 78 rpm disks that could hold only 3 minutes of music? The LP held a total of 60 minutes of music over its 2 sides, while today's CDs make 78 minutes of music possible on one disk!

# Parmesan-Baked Tomatoes

Tomatoes—they're perfect in our salads, cooked down in our sauces, and even baked as a special go-along to liven up our dinner plates! And this is just how tomatoes were prepared as a popular side dish in the '60s and '70s.

    ½ cup Italian-flavored bread crumbs
    3 tablespoons butter, melted
    ⅛ teaspoon black pepper
    3 large tomatoes, each cut crosswise in half
    1 tablespoon grated Parmesan cheese

Preheat the oven to 350°F. In a small bowl, combine the bread crumbs, butter, and pepper; mix well. Place the tomatoes in an 8-inch square baking dish. Pat the filling mixture evenly over the cut side of each tomato half. Sprinkle with the Parmesan cheese and bake for 18 to 20 minutes, or until the topping is golden and the tomatoes are heated through. Serve immediately.

# Zucchini and Tomato Bake

*Quality* time?! All I hear from everybody today is, "There's *no* time!" But maybe, just maybe, if we had some old-fashioned-tasting comfort foods that were today-easy to make, we'd tempt that gang of ours to cut short all those extra activities—maybe even once a week. And then we could sit down at the table and enjoy a quality meal— and quality time—together.

>   3 medium zucchini, cut into ¼-inch-thick slices
>   1 can (28 ounces) diced tomatoes, drained
>   1 medium onion, thinly sliced
>   1 teaspoon dried oregano
>   ½ teaspoon garlic powder
>   ½ teaspoon salt
>   ¼ teaspoon black pepper
>   ¼ cup grated Parmesan cheese

Preheat the oven to 400°F. Coat an 8-inch square baking dish with nonstick cooking spray. In a large bowl, combine all the ingredients except the Parmesan cheese; mix well. Spoon into the baking dish and sprinkle with the Parmesan cheese. Bake for 30 to 35 minutes, or until the zucchini is tender. Serve immediately.

# Vegetable Cornucopia

*6 servings*

It's time to come home to the tastes of the good old USA. Yes, our traditional horn of plenty, the cornucopia, is brimming with tasty veggies!

  ¼ cup (½ stick) butter
  ½ pound fresh baby carrots
  1 teaspoon dried dillweed
  ½ teaspoon salt
  ¼ teaspoon black pepper
  1 medium onion, thinly sliced
  2 medium yellow squash, cut into 1-inch chunks
  1 medium zucchini, cut into 1-inch chunks
  1 can (8 ounces) sliced water chestnuts, drained

Melt the butter in a medium saucepan over medium-high heat. Add the carrots, dillweed, salt, and pepper; mix well. Sauté for 10 minutes, or until crisp-tender, stirring occasionally. Add the onion and sauté for 2 minutes. Add the remaining ingredients and sauté for 2 to 3 minutes, or until the vegetables are tender. Serve immediately.

***Note:*** If you have fresh dill on hand, you might want to chop and add 1 to 2 tablespoons of it in place of the dried.

# Peachy-Keen Potatoes, Rice, and Noodles

| | |
|---|---|
| Creamy Potatoes au Gratin | 109 |
| Rosemary Roasted Potatoes | 110 |
| Piled-High Mashed Potatoes | 111 |
| Wow-'Em Cheese Fries | 112 |
| Tiny Taters | 113 |
| Whipped Potatoes Plus | 114 |
| Skillet Sweet Potatoes | 115 |
| Nothing-to-It Sweet Potatoes | 116 |
| Memory-Making Homemade Noodles | 117 |
| Special Spaetzle | 118 |
| Home-Style Macaroni and Cheese | 119 |
| Fast-and-Cheap Browned Noodles | 120 |
| Picture-Perfect Noodle Ring | 121 |
| Piña Colada Rice | 122 |
| Take-out–Style Veggie Fried Rice | 123 |
| Speedy Almond Rice | 124 |
| Cheddar Rice Bake | 125 |
| Zippy Corn Bread Dressing | 126 |

# Creamy Potatoes au Gratin

It wasn't that long ago that there was no such thing as packaged shredded cheese available in the supermarket dairy section. We had to shred it by hand! Nowadays we can buy it already done, and that's such a help when we want to make this creamy side dish!

½ cup milk
1 teaspoon Italian seasoning
1 teaspoon onion powder
½ teaspoon salt
¼ teaspoon white pepper
5 large potatoes (about 2 pounds), peeled and cut into
    ¼-inch-thick slices
2 tablespoons butter, cut into small pieces
½ cup (2 ounces) shredded Cheddar cheese, divided
2 tablespoons grated Parmesan cheese
¼ teaspoon paprika

Preheat the oven to 350°F. Coat an 8-inch square baking dish with nonstick cooking spray. In a small bowl, combine the milk, Italian seasoning, onion powder, salt, and white pepper; mix well. Arrange the potato slices in the baking dish. Pour the milk mixture over them, then dot with the butter. Cover with aluminum foil and bake for 1 hour, or until the potatoes are tender. Uncover and sprinkle with the cheeses and paprika. Bake uncovered for 5 to 8 minutes, or until the cheeses melt. Serve immediately.

*Note:* Try this with red potatoes for a change of pace—just scrub well and slice them with the skins on. Sprinkle the casserole with chopped fresh parsley just before serving.

# Rosemary Roasted Potatoes

*6 servings*

Once upon a time, salt and pepper were pretty much the only season-ings used in most American recipes. Herbs and spices were consid-ered fancy. Fortunately, we've gotten a lot more adventurous and now we can find both the fresh and dried varieties of most herbs right at our local supermarkets. So let's take advantage of the availability of rosemary and parsley for these flavor-packed potatoes!

> 2 pounds small red potatoes, scrubbed and quartered
> ½ cup (1 stick) butter, melted
> 1 teaspoon dried rosemary (see Note)
> ½ teaspoon salt
> ¼ teaspoon black pepper
> 2 tablespoons chopped fresh parsley

Preheat the oven to 325°F. Coat an 8-inch square baking dish with nonstick cooking spray. In a large bowl, combine all the ingredients except the parsley; mix well. Pour into the baking dish and bake for 1¼ to 1½ hours, or until the potatoes are fork-tender. Sprinkle with the parsley and serve.

***Note:*** If you have fresh rosemary on hand, you can replace the dried with 1 to 2 tablespoons chopped fresh rosemary. Remember—any time you replace dried herbs with fresh, it takes 1 tablespoon of the fresh to replace 1 teaspoon of the dried.

# Piled-High Mashed Potatoes

Walk into a diner and order meat loaf or fried chicken and you'll get a bonus piled on your plate. I'm talking about a pile of mashed potatoes. It seems like the ones we get today are creamier and tastier than ever. And it's not unusual for them to be colorful, too, 'cause the potato peels are mixed right in. (That's my favorite way!)

> 8 medium red potatoes (about 3 pounds), scrubbed and
>     cut into large chunks
> ½ cup sour cream
> ¼ cup milk
> 1 teaspoon salt
> ½ teaspoon black pepper
> 1 jar (12 ounces) mushroom gravy, warmed

Place the potatoes in a large pot and add enough water to cover them. Bring to a boil over high heat. Reduce the heat to medium and cook for 20 to 25 minutes, or until fork-tender; drain. In a large bowl, combine the potatoes, sour cream, milk, salt, and pepper; beat until smooth and well blended. Serve with the warmed gravy.

*Note:* To peel or not to peel? That's always the question. I like mashed potatoes best with the peel left on for color and texture, plus that's where the nutrients are—but make them the way your gang prefers.

# Wow-'Em Cheese Fries

Forget the tortilla chips—these hearty '90s nacho-style fries are smothered in a '50s favorite—easy-to-use Cheez Whiz!

> 1 package (32 ounces) frozen French fries (see Note)
> ¾ cup Cheez Whiz, melted
> ½ cup salsa
> 2 tablespoons real bacon bits

Preheat the oven to 450°F. Spread the French fries evenly on a large rimmed baking sheet. Bake for 20 to 25 minutes, or until golden brown. Mound the cooked French fries on a serving platter and top with the melted cheese, salsa, and bacon bits. Serve immediately.

*Note:* Make sure to use regular plain fries—not a coated, crinkle-cut, or shoestring variety. The traditional ones look and taste best with these toppings.

# Tiny Taters

There's no denying it. Every decade has its own flavor—in food as well as music. Elvis of the '50s and early '60s gave way to the British invasion of the Beatles and the Rolling Stones. Since then, there have been a few more waves to make the scene. And with each one, there were new dances—disco, the hustle, the mashed potato. . . . And, speaking of potatoes, here's one with an easy "twist"!

   3 cups prepared warm mashed potatoes (see Note)
   2 egg yolks, beaten

Preheat the oven to 400°F. Coat a large rimmed baking sheet with nonstick cooking spray. Using your hands, roll the mashed potatoes into small nuggets. Flatten each end and place on the cookie sheet. Brush the top and sides of each with the egg yolks. Bake for 25 to 30 minutes, or until golden brown. Serve immediately.

***Note:*** You can make your own mashed potatoes or just whip up a batch of instant mashed potatoes. Just remember to season them the way you like 'em.

# Whipped Potatoes Plus

Years ago, we made plain mashed potatoes with butter and milk. Then came the ones that had roasted garlic. Well, there have been lots of other varieties since those cropped up, but lately I've been making them with parsnips and onions to give the potatoes an extra-rich taste. Who knows . . . we might be starting a whole new trend right here!

    6 large potatoes (about 3 pounds), peeled and quartered
    6 medium parsnips, peeled and cut into 1-inch chunks
    2 medium onions, cut into 8 wedges each
    4 garlic cloves, peeled
    1 cup sour cream
    1½ teaspoons salt
    ¼ teaspoon black pepper

Place the potatoes, parsnips, onions, and garlic in a soup pot and add enough water to cover them. Cover and bring to a boil over medium-high heat; reduce the heat to medium-low and cook for 18 to 20 minutes, or until the vegetables are tender. Drain and transfer to a large bowl. Add the sour cream, salt, and pepper and beat for 3 to 4 minutes, or until creamy. Serve.

**Note:** It's no problem making these a day or two before serving them. Just keep them ready in the fridge so all you have to do is heat 'em in the microwave for a few minutes before mealtime.

# Skillet Sweet Potatoes

Let's get out of the side dish blues! There *is* life beyond mashed, baked, and French-fried white potatoes!

>  ¼ cup (½ stick) butter
>  4 medium sweet potatoes (about 2 pounds), peeled and thinly
>      sliced
>  ½ teaspoon salt
>  1 can (6 ounces) pineapple juice
>  2 tablespoons all-purpose flour

Melt the butter in a large skillet over medium heat. Add the sweet potatoes and salt. Cover and cook for 18 to 20 minutes, or until tender, stirring occasionally. In a small bowl, combine the pineapple juice and flour; mix well and pour over the potatoes. Cook for 1 to 2 minutes, or until thickened, stirring frequently. Serve immediately.

***Note:*** Sometimes I like to use more butter and sauté the potato slices in batches to get them nice and brown before covering and cooking until tender.

# Nothing-to-It Sweet Potatoes

---

## 6 servings

---

Potlucks, progressive dinners, or "bring a dish" parties—we've all been invited to one of them. And whatever name we gave them, they were a fun way to get together with friends for an evening of good food and good company. They really are fun and, if they're done right, they can be easy for everybody. So why not invite some friends over for a potluck supper—but tell them *you're* making the mashed sweet potatoes.

> 2 cans (29 ounces each) sweet potatoes or yams,
>    drained and mashed
> Juice of ½ orange
> 2 tablespoons butter

In a soup pot, combine all the ingredients over medium heat; mix well. Cook for 5 to 7 minutes, or until smooth and heated through, stirring occasionally. Serve immediately, or transfer to a serving dish and let cool, then cover and chill. Rewarm in a 325°F. oven for about 30 minutes before serving.

**Note:** How about adding an extra touch of sweetness by stirring in a tablespoon or two of brown sugar and a sprinkle of cinnamon?

# Memory-Making Homemade Noodles

---

## 4 to 6 servings

---

It's true what they say—there really is no place like home. Whether we live in a small cottage, on a farm, in a big-city high-rise, or in a sprawling suburban ranch house, home is the place we all head to for comfort. And, very often, our favorite memories are connected to what was often waiting there for us to eat—like a big bowl of soup full of homemade noodles. Mmm!

2½ cups all-purpose flour
2 eggs
⅓ cup milk
1 tablespoon chopped fresh parsley
1 teaspoon salt
¼ cup (½ stick) butter

In a large bowl, combine all the ingredients except the butter; mix until a stiff dough forms. On a lightly floured work surface, roll the dough out to form a 16" × 20" rectangle. Cut into ¼" × 5" strips and allow to sit for 15 minutes. Meanwhile, bring a soup pot of water to a boil over high heat. Drop about half the noodles into the boiling water and cook for 10 to 12 minutes, or until tender, stirring frequently. With a slotted spoon, remove the noodles to a colander to drain. Repeat with the remaining noodles. Toss with the butter and serve immediately.

*Note:* Make sure to stir the noodles as you drop them into the boiling water to keep them from sticking together.

---

# Special Spaetzle

What a melting pot we live in! Our American culture and everything from how we talk and dress to how we eat has been built on the influences of Italian, Spanish, Irish, and other cultures. Take this homemade German noodle . . . it's more popular than ever!

3 cups all-purpose flour
½ teaspoon baking powder
2 teaspoons salt, divided
¼ teaspoon black pepper
4 eggs, beaten
1 cup water

In a large bowl, combine the flour, baking powder, 1 teaspoon salt, and the pepper; mix well. Add the eggs and water; mix until smooth. Fill a soup pot half-full with water and add the remaining 1 teaspoon salt; bring to a boil over high heat. In batches, drizzle the batter from a spoon into the boiling water. When the spaetzle (noodles) float to the top of the water, remove them with a slotted spoon and drain in a colander. Serve warm.

*Note:* These make a great side to any meal served as is or tossed with melted butter and chopped fresh parsley.

# Home-Style Macaroni and Cheese

*6 servings*

Moms of yesterday and today have one big thing in common—how much they care about what their families eat. I mean, aren't moms always trying to please everybody with tasty main dishes like this hearty homemade mac and cheese?!

1 pound elbow macaroni
¼ cup (½ stick) butter
2 tablespoons all-purpose flour
1 teaspoon salt
½ teaspoon black pepper
2 cups milk
4 cups (16 ounces) shredded sharp Cheddar cheese

Preheat the oven to 375°F. Coat a 9" × 13" baking dish with nonstick cooking spray. Cook the macaroni according to the package directions; drain and place half in the bottom of the baking dish. Melt the butter in a medium saucepan over medium heat. Add the flour, salt, and pepper; stir to mix well. Gradually add the milk; bring to a boil and cook until smooth and thickened, stirring constantly. Sprinkle 1½ cups cheese over the macaroni in the baking dish and top with half of the white sauce. Repeat the layers once more, then top with the remaining 1 cup cheese. Bake for 35 to 40 minutes, or until heated through and the top is golden. Serve immediately.

# Fast-and-Cheap Browned Noodles

Remember the cars of yesterday? They didn't have air-conditioning or fancy stereos or CD players. They were just basic cars that got us from place to place—and they did that . . . really well. So that reminds me that, like these noodles, sometimes basic is best.

> 2 tablespoons vegetable oil
> 2 packages (3 ounces each) chicken-flavored ramen
>     noodles
> 2 cups water

Heat the oil in a large skillet over medium-high heat. Break up the noodles and add to the skillet, cooking until browned, stirring constantly. Add the noodle seasoning packets and water; cook until all the water is absorbed and the noodles are tender, stirring occasionally. Serve immediately.

## Did You Know . . .

Back in the 1950s, guys who loved working on their cars were called "greasers" or "motorheads" and the "cool cats" and "hip chicks" were the ones winning popularity contests?

# Picture-Perfect Noodle Ring

This one's a "dead ringer" for a favorite cake shape—but today, it doubles as a centerpiece and a tasty go-along for our main course. It's perfect as the base for Chicken à la King (page 59) and other saucy favorites.

    1 package (8 ounces) fine egg noodles
    1 cup (4 ounces) shredded Cheddar cheese
    ¼ cup ketchup
    1 tablespoon butter
    1 tablespoon Worcestershire sauce
    ½ teaspoon salt
    3 eggs, beaten

Preheat the oven to 350°F. Prepare the noodles according to the package directions; drain. Coat a 10-inch Bundt pan with nonstick cooking spray. In a large saucepan, combine the cheese, ketchup, and butter over medium-low heat, stirring until the cheese and butter are completely melted. Remove from the heat and stir in the Worcestershire sauce and salt. Add the noodles and the beaten eggs; mix well and spoon into the Bundt pan, packing down lightly. Bake for 25 to 30 minutes, or until firm and light golden. Allow to sit for 5 minutes, then carefully invert onto a serving platter and serve.

# Piña Colada Rice

Remember those themed backyard luaus and beach bashes of the 1960s? The food sure was yummy. Barbecued kebabs, fruity drinks, and savory sides like this fluffy white rice can still make any party a tropical delight.

> 1 cup piña colada drink mix
> 1 can (8 ounces) crushed pineapple, undrained
> ½ cup water
> ½ teaspoon salt
> ⅛ teaspoon ground red pepper
> 2 cups instant rice
> 1 jar (2 ounces) chopped pimientos, drained

In a medium saucepan, combine the piña colada mix, crushed pineapple with its juice, water, salt, and ground red pepper; mix well and bring to a boil over high heat. Stir in the rice. Remove from the heat, cover, and allow to sit for 5 minutes, or until the liquid is absorbed. Add the pimientos; mix well and serve immediately.

*Note:* For even more color, stir in 2 tablespoons chopped fresh parsley at the same time as the pimientos.

# Take-out-Style Veggie Fried Rice

Think back a bit—remember the very first time you ever set foot in a Chinese restaurant? Back in the '50s, Chinese food first became really big here. We "Americanized" a lot of it and whatever we did stuck, 'cause today it's as popular as ever—and easier than ever to make at home, too!

> 2 tablespoons plus 2 teaspoons vegetable oil, divided
> 2 eggs, lightly beaten
> 1 package (16 ounces) frozen peas and carrots, thawed
> 3 cups cold cooked rice
> ¼ cup soy sauce

Heat 2 teaspoons vegetable oil in a large skillet over medium-high heat. Add the eggs and scramble. Break the egg up into small pieces; remove from the skillet and set aside. Heat the remaining 2 tablespoons oil in the same skillet; add the peas and carrots and cook for 3 minutes. Add the rice and soy sauce and cook for 3 to 5 minutes, or until heated through, stirring frequently. Stir in the scrambled eggs and cook for 1 to 2 minutes, or until heated through. Serve immediately.

*Note:* This is a great dish to make when you have leftover rice—or the next time you make rice, just make extra so you'll have some ready to go for this dish.

# Speedy Almond Rice

---

### 4 to 6 servings

---

They'll be nuts about this fancy-tasting go-along. And with our "instant" helpers to speed things up, we'll want to enjoy it again and again!

> 1 tablespoon vegetable oil
> ½ cup fine egg noodles
> ¼ cup slivered almonds (see Note)
> 2½ cups water
> 2 cups instant rice
> 1 teaspoon salt

Heat the oil in a large skillet over medium-low heat. Add the noodles and almonds and cook until golden brown (be careful—they brown quickly). Add the remaining ingredients, increase the heat to medium-high, and bring to a boil, stirring occasionally. Cover and remove from the heat. Allow to stand for 5 minutes, or until all the liquid is absorbed. Fluff with a fork and serve.

**Note:** If you'd rather make this without the nuts, that's fine—just leave them out.

# Cheddar Rice Bake

Is it rice or is it a casserole? It's a little of both and a whole lotta good taste, 'cause the instant rice makes it an instant success.

1½ cups instant rice
1½ cups milk
¼ cup (½ stick) butter, melted
¼ cup shredded white Cheddar cheese
⅓ cup finely chopped fresh parsley
2 eggs
½ teaspoon onion powder
½ teaspoon salt
⅛ teaspoon black pepper

Preheat the oven to 350°F. Coat an 8-inch square baking dish with nonstick cooking spray. In a large bowl, combine all the ingredients; mix well. Pour into the baking dish and bake for 30 to 35 minutes, or until golden and the rice is tender. Serve immediately.

# Zippy Corn Bread Dressing

---

### 6 servings

---

Think corn bread dressing is a pain to make? Well, no more! 'Cause now I've got a bunch of shortcuts that'll guarantee it'll zip right along!

  1 can (10½ ounces) condensed chicken broth
  1¼ cups water
  ½ cup (1 stick) butter
  1 package (16 ounces) corn bread stuffing
  1 can (11 ounces) Mexican-style corn, drained

Preheat the oven to 350°F. In a soup pot, combine the chicken broth, water, and butter and bring to a boil over high heat. Add the stuffing, then remove from the heat; mix well. Stir in the corn, then spoon into a 3-quart casserole dish. Cover and bake for 20 to 25 minutes, or until heated through. Serve immediately.

***Note:*** It's really great that this dressing doesn't have to cook too long, because if you're making it to go along with a turkey, you can remove the turkey from the oven and bake this while the turkey is standing.

# Dazzlin' Desserts

Daffodil Cake 129

Shortcut German Chocolate Cake 130

Lemon Meringue Cake 131

Sour Cream Coffee Cake 132

Chocolate Polka-dot Cake 133

Chocolate-Raspberry Cheesecake 134

Boston Cream Pie 135

Strawberry-Rhubarb Pie 136

Easy-Crust Custard Pie 137

Peanut Butter Pie 138

Almond Toffee Brownies 139

M&M Drop Cookies 140

Half-Moon Cookies 141

Cornflake Cookies 142

Show-off Glazed Doughnuts 143

Pure and Simple Vanilla Ice Cream 144

No-Bake Baked Alaska 145

Strawberry Snowballs 146

Good Fortune Sherbet 147

Old-fashioned Tortoni 148

Frozen Chocolate—Coconut Mounds     149
Simple Peach Melba     150
Coffee Bavarian Crème     151
Apple-Raisin Tarts     152
Blueberry Betty     153
Apricot Bread Pudding     154
Cherry-Pineapple Crumb Cobbler     155
Soda Fountain Hot Fudge     156

# Daffodil Cake

Angel food cake is an oldie but goodie made either from scratch or a shortcut easy way, like this one. And when we add a dash of sunshine . . . oh boy! It looks as good as it tastes!

> 1 package (16 ounces) angel food cake mix, batter prepared
>    according to the package directions
> ⅛ teaspoon yellow food color
> Grated peel of 1 lemon

Preheat the oven to 350°F. Divide the batter in half and add the yellow food color and lemon peel to one half; mix well, until the batter turns yellow. Drop a tablespoon of white batter into a 10-inch tube pan, drop a tablespoon of yellow batter next to it, and continue alternating tablespoons of each batter until the bottom of the pan is completely covered. Continue with the remaining batter, dropping tablespoons of the white batter over the white batter and yellow batter over the yellow batter. Bake according to the package directions for a tube pan. Remove from the oven and invert the pan until completely cool. Remove the cake from the pan by running a knife around the edge of the pan to loosen it and inverting onto a serving platter.

***Note:*** Wanna fancy this up? Top it with a glaze made of 1 cup confectioners' sugar mixed with 2 tablespoons fresh lemon juice.

# Shortcut German Chocolate Cake

*12 to 16 servings*

To enjoy this one, we don't have to worry about remembering our tickets and passports, 'cause right in our own kitchens we'll be transported to the land of rich, nutty chocolate cake.

    1 package (18¼ ounces) German chocolate cake mix, batter
        prepared according to the package directions
    1 cup chopped pecans, divided
    1 cup sweetened flaked coconut, divided
    1 can (14 ounces) sweetened condensed milk
    3 tablespoons butter
    1 teaspoon vanilla extract

Preheat the oven to 350°F. Coat three 8-inch round cake pans with nonstick cooking spray. Add ½ cup pecans and ½ cup coconut to the cake batter; mix well. Pour into the cake pans and bake for 22 to 25 minutes, or until a wooden toothpick inserted in the center comes out clean. Allow to cool slightly, then remove to a wire rack to cool completely. In a small saucepan, combine the sweetened condensed milk, butter, and vanilla over medium heat. Cook for 3 to 4 minutes, or until thickened, stirring constantly. Stir in the remaining ½ cup pecans and ½ cup coconut. Place one cake layer on a serving platter and spread with one third of the frosting. Top with the remaining layers, frosting the top of each one; do not frost the sides. Serve at room temperature. Cover and chill any leftovers.

***Note:*** If you don't have three 8-inch round cake pans, use two 9-inch round cake pans and frost as a 2-layer cake. Or simply bake it in a 9" × 13" pan and frost the top.

# Lemon Meringue Cake

No, the title of this recipe isn't a mistake—it's a cake all right, but with the same light and zesty taste of the pie we grew up loving.

    1 teaspoon grated lemon peel
    1 package (18¼ ounces) lemon cake mix, batter prepared
        according to the package directions
    4 egg whites
    ¼ teaspoon salt
    1 cup sugar

Preheat the oven to 350°F. Coat a 9" × 13" baking dish with nonstick cooking spray. Stir the lemon peel into the cake batter and pour into the baking dish. In a medium bowl, beat the egg whites and salt until soft peaks form. Gradually beat in the sugar until stiff peaks form. Spoon over the cake batter, carefully spreading to completely cover the batter. Make sure to form lots of peaks and valleys with a spatula to create a tempting-looking meringue. Bake for 40 to 45 minutes, or until the meringue is golden and a wooden toothpick inserted in the center of the cake comes out clean. Allow to cool completely, then cut into squares and serve.

*Note:* This can also be made as two 9-inch round cakes. Just pour the batter into two cake pans and spread each with the meringue mixture.

# Sour Cream Coffee Cake

Coffee cake is something that's never gone out of style. Sprinkled with cinnamon and nuts or mixed with apples and cranberries, it gives us an excuse to eat cake for breakfast . . . or any other time of the day!

    1 cup chopped walnuts
    ⅓ cup sugar
    2 teaspoons ground cinnamon
    1 package (18¼ ounces) yellow cake mix
    1 cup sour cream
    1 cup water
    2 eggs

Preheat the oven to 350°F. Coat a 9" × 13" baking dish with nonstick cooking spray. In a medium bowl, combine the walnuts, sugar, and cinnamon; mix well and set aside. In a large bowl, beat the cake mix, sour cream, water, and eggs until well combined. Spread half the batter in the baking dish and sprinkle with half the nut mixture, then repeat the layers. Bake for 25 to 30 minutes, or until a wooden toothpick inserted in the center comes out clean. Allow to cool slightly, then cut into squares and serve warm; or allow to cool completely before serving.

***Note:*** This can also be made in two 9-inch round cake pans—then there's one to enjoy now and one to freeze for enjoying later.

# Chocolate Polka-dot Cake

This one really takes the cake, 'cause it not only tastes great, but it looks great, too!

 1 package (18¼ ounces) devil's food cake mix
 1 cup water
 ⅓ cup chocolate-flavored syrup
 ⅓ cup vegetable oil
 3 eggs
 ¾ cup (4½ ounces) semisweet chocolate chips, divided
 ½ cup (1 stick) butter, softened
 ½ cup plus ½ teaspoon vegetable shortening
 4 cups confectioners' sugar
 2 tablespoons milk
 1 teaspoon vanilla extract

Preheat the oven to 325°F. Coat two 9-inch round cake pans with non-stick cooking spray. In a large bowl, combine the cake mix, water, chocolate syrup, oil, and eggs; beat well. Stir in ½ cup chocolate chips, then pour into the pans. Bake for 35 to 40 minutes, or until a wooden toothpick inserted in the center comes out clean. Allow to cool for 10 minutes, then invert onto wire racks to cool completely. In a medium bowl, beat the butter, ½ cup vegetable shortening, confectioners' sugar, milk, and vanilla until light and fluffy; frost the cake. Melt the remaining chocolate chips and vegetable shortening in a small saucepan over low heat, stirring constantly. Allow to cool slightly, then dip the back of a teaspoon into the melted chocolate and make chocolate polka dots all over the cake by swirling the back of the spoon into the white frosting. Serve, or cover loosely until ready to serve.

# Chocolate-Raspberry Cheesecake

*8 to 10 servings*

Remember the taste of old-fashioned deli-style creamy cheesecake? Imagine adding two popular tastes to it . . . ! Actually, now you don't have to imagine—you can just dig in!

2 cups crushed cream-filled chocolate sandwich cookies
¼ cup (½ stick) butter, melted
2 packages (8 ounces each) cream cheese, softened
2 eggs
¾ cup sugar
½ cup (3 ounces) semisweet chocolate chips, melted
⅓ cup seedless raspberry preserves

Preheat the oven to 325°F. In a medium bowl, combine the crushed chocolate sandwich cookies and melted butter; mix well and press into the bottom and up the sides of a 9-inch deep-dish pie plate to form a crust. In a large bowl, beat the cream cheese, eggs, and sugar until smooth. Reserve ⅓ cup of the mixture and set aside in a small bowl. Pour the remaining mixture into the prepared crust. Add the melted chocolate and the raspberry preserves to the reserved cream cheese mixture; mix well and drop by spoonfuls into the mixture in the crust. Swirl with a knife to create a marbled effect. Bake for 50 to 55 minutes, or until almost set in the center. Allow to cool for 1 hour, then cover and chill for at least 6 hours before serving.

***Note:*** It's nice to add a bit of color to this by garnishing each serving with a dollop of whipped cream, some fresh raspberries, and a sprig of mint.

# Boston Cream Pie

Did you know that traditional Boston cream pie really isn't a pie at all? It's a round layer cake with a custard filling and chocolate topping. You're gonna love it so much, you won't care what it's called!

> 1 package (18¼ ounces) yellow cake mix, batter prepared according to the package directions
> 1 package (4-serving size) instant vanilla pudding and pie filling
> 1 cup milk
> ¼ cup sugar
> 2 teaspoons cornstarch
> ⅓ cup water
> ½ ounce (½ square) unsweetened chocolate
> ½ teaspoon vanilla extract

Bake the cake batter according to the package directions for two 8-inch round cake pans; let cool. Reserve 1 cake layer for later use (see Note). Slice the remaining cake layer horizontally in half and place the bottom half cut side up on a serving plate. In a medium bowl, whisk the pudding mix and milk together until thick and smooth; spread over the bottom cake layer. Place the remaining half cake layer cut side down over the pudding. Chill while preparing the chocolate glaze. In a small saucepan, combine the sugar, cornstarch, water, and chocolate over low heat; cook until the chocolate is melted and the mixture is thick and smooth, stirring constantly. Remove from the heat and stir in the vanilla. Allow to cool slightly, then spread over the top of the cake. Chill for at least 1 hour, or until the filling and glaze are set, before serving.

**Note:** This one starts with a cake mix, so you'll be making an extra cake layer.

# Strawberry-Rhubarb Pie

## 6 servings

When we were kids, most of us probably thought, "Rhubarb—yuck!" It wasn't until we grew up and began trying more foods that we realized we were missing out. Be sure you don't miss out on this one!

    1 quart strawberries, washed, hulled, and quartered
    1 cup sugar
    1 package (15 ounces) folded refrigerated pie crusts,
        at room temperature
    1 cup cubed fresh rhubarb (see Note)
    ⅓ cup all-purpose flour
    1 tablespoon butter, melted

Preheat the oven to 425°F. In a large bowl, combine the strawberries and sugar; mix well, until the sugar dissolves. Unfold 1 pie crust and place in a 9-inch deep-dish pie plate, pressing the crust firmly into the plate. Place the remaining pie crust on a work surface and, using the plastic cap of a soda bottle, cut 8 to 10 circles from the center, forming polka dots, leaving a 2-inch border around the edges. Add the remaining ingredients to the strawberry mixture; mix well and spoon into the pie crust. Place the cut-out crust over the strawberry mixture. Pinch together and trim the edges to seal, then flute, if desired. Bake for 30 to 35 minutes, or until the crust is golden and the filling is bubbly. Allow to cool slightly before serving, or chill until ready to serve.

*Note:* If fresh rhubarb is not in season, you can substitute a cup of frozen rhubarb that you've thawed and drained.

# Easy-Crust Custard Pie

No time to bake a pie from scratch? Today's busy schedules often keep us from doing things we love, like baking homemade treats for the family. Well, today we've got plenty of shortcuts, like ready-to-bake pie shells, to help us.

> 2 cups applesauce
> ¾ cup sugar
> 3 eggs
> 3 tablespoons butter, melted
> 2 tablespoons fresh lemon juice
> 1½ teaspoons all-purpose flour
> 1 teaspoon grated lemon peel
> ¼ teaspoon salt
> One 9-inch frozen ready-to-bake deep-dish pie shell, thawed

Preheat the oven to 350°F. In a large bowl, combine all the ingredients except the pie shell; mix well. Pour into the pie shell and bake for 60 to 70 minutes, or until light golden and the center is set. Allow to cool, then cover and chill for at least 2 hours before serving.

***Note:*** Make sure when you are grating the lemon peel to grate only the yellow part of the peel, not the bitter white pith.

# Peanut Butter Pie

Want some real quality time? Try making some things in advance, then sit back and enjoy the family instead of rushing around the kitchen and missing all the fun! Whip up this peanutty pie the night before—then all you have to do is keep it chilled till after dinner!

> 1 package (6-serving size) instant vanilla pudding and
>     pie filling
> 1½ cups milk
> 1 cup creamy peanut butter
> One 9-inch chocolate graham cracker pie crust
> 1 container (8 ounces) frozen whipped topping, thawed
> 2 tablespoons coarsely chopped peanuts

In a large bowl, whisk the pudding mix and milk until well combined. Add the peanut butter and continue whisking until smooth. Spoon into the pie crust. Spread the whipped topping over the peanut butter mixture and sprinkle with the chopped peanuts. Cover and chill for at least 2 hours, or until the pudding is set.

***Note:*** To make this a crunchy peanut butter pie, use crunchy peanut butter in place of the creamy. If you prefer to add a bit of chocolate flavor, garnish it with miniature semisweet chocolate chips sprinkled over the whipped topping.

# Almond Toffee Brownies

---

## 12 to 15 squares

---

Some of us remember often finding Mom waiting at home for us after school with a plate full of hot-out-of-the-oven brownies and a tall glass of milk. We'd enjoy a rich homemade snack before starting our homework. Well, today's moms still do that for their kids—but often with help from convenience items. (And the kids have help, too, from calculators and computers!)

> ¾ cup slivered almonds
> 1 package (19.8 ounces) brownie mix, batter prepared
>     according to the package directions
> Two (1.4 ounces each) chocolate-covered toffee bars, crushed

Preheat the oven to 350°F. Coat a 9" × 13" baking pan with nonstick cooking spray. Add the almonds to the brownie batter; mix well and pour into the baking pan. Sprinkle with the crushed candy bars. Bake according to the package directions for a 9" × 13" baking pan. Allow to cool; cut into squares and serve.

***Note:*** Do not refrigerate these. Instead, store in an airtight container at room temperature. That way, the toffee bits will stay soft and gooey.

# M&M Drop Cookies

At one time, there was only one kind of M&M's—the plain ones. Nowadays we can find them in peanut, almond, mint, and peanut butter varieties . . . plus lots of new colors and sizes, too. What a welcome addition they all are to our baking!

   1 package (18¼ ounces) white cake mix
   ⅓ cup vegetable oil
   2 eggs
   ¾ cup miniature M&M's baking bits

Preheat the oven to 350°F. Coat two cookie sheets with nonstick cooking spray. In a large bowl, beat the cake mix, oil, and eggs for 3 to 4 minutes, or until well blended. Using a spoon, stir in the M&M's baking bits. Drop by teaspoonfuls 2 inches apart onto the cookie sheets. Bake for 10 to 12 minutes, or until firm and golden around the edges. Allow to cool for 3 to 4 minutes, then remove to wire racks to cool completely. Serve, or store in an airtight container until ready to serve.

## Did You Know . . .

M&M's candies were created to overcome the problem of chocolate melting in the stores in warmer months? With their chocolate centers encased in a colorful sugar coating, M&M's could stand up to heat, making chocolate available year-round!

# Half-Moon Cookies

about 1½ dozen cookies

Remember those big half-vanilla, half-chocolate cookies that all the bakeries and supermarkets sold when we were kids? Whether you called them half-and-halfs, black-and-whites, or half-moons, you can still enjoy their yummy taste with the help of this easy recipe.

    1 package (18¼ ounces) white cake mix (see Note)
    ⅓ cup vegetable oil
    2 eggs
    8 ounces (½ a 16-ounce container) chocolate frosting
    8 ounces (½ a 16-ounce container) vanilla frosting

Preheat the oven to 350°F. Coat two cookie sheets with nonstick cooking spray. In a large bowl, combine the cake mix, oil, and eggs; mix well. Drop by heaping tablespoonfuls 2 inches apart onto the cookie sheets. Bake for 12 to 14 minutes, or until firm. Remove to wire racks to cool completely. Frost half of the flat side of each cookie with vanilla frosting and the other half with chocolate frosting. Serve, or loosely cover until ready to serve.

*Note:* To make chocolate half-moon cookies, simply use chocolate cake mix.

# Cornflake Cookies

To many of us, cookies are the perfect dessert, 'cause we don't need forks or plates to eat them. And these yummy cookies go with everything. They're not too sweet, and they get their crunch from a cereal that's been a favorite for decades!

> 2 egg whites
> 1 cup packed light brown sugar
> 1 teaspoon vanilla extract
> 4 cups cornflake cereal (see Note)
> 1 cup chopped pecans

Preheat the oven to 275°F. Coat two cookie sheets with nonstick cooking spray. In a medium bowl, beat the egg whites until foamy. Continue beating and gradually add the brown sugar and vanilla; beat until stiff peaks form. Fold in the cornflakes and pecans until evenly distributed. Drop by rounded tablespoons 1 inch apart onto the baking sheets and bake for 20 minutes. Turn the oven off and leave the cookies in the oven for 15 more minutes, or until firm in the center and light golden. Allow to cool completely and then serve, or store in an airtight container until ready to serve.

***Note:*** If you have no cornflakes on hand, you can use almost any cold cereal—but make sure it's not a sweetened variety, or the cookies will be overly sweet.

# Show-off Glazed Doughnuts

Wanna really show off? Make your own doughnuts! Yup, with every-body into making homemade breads and ice cream, why not dough-nuts, too? Once you taste 'em fresh out of the pan, store-bought will be a thing of the past!

> 2⅓ cups confectioners' sugar
> 3 tablespoons water
> Vegetable oil for cooking
> 2 packages (4½ ounces each) refrigerated biscuits
>   (6 biscuits each)

In a small bowl, combine the confectioners' sugar and water; mix well and set aside. In a soup pot, heat 1 inch of oil over high heat until hot but not smoking. Separate the biscuits and lay on a cutting board. Using an apple corer or a sharp knife, cut out a small circle from the center of each biscuit, forming doughnut shapes. Cook in batches in the hot oil for about 1 minute per side, or until golden brown. Drain on a paper towel–lined baking sheet. While still hot, dip in the confectioners' sugar glaze, turning to coat completely. Place on a wire rack that has been placed over a baking sheet to drain. Serve warm.

***Note:*** For chocolate-glazed doughnuts, add 1 tablespoon unsweet-ened cocoa to the glaze. Don't forget to cook the donut "holes," too!

# Pure and Simple Vanilla Ice Cream

---

*about 1 pint*

---

Yes, we can make premium-style ice cream in our kitchens with just a few ingredients and an electric mixer! Who knew something this good could be so easy? (We did, of course!)

> 1 can (14 ounces) sweetened condensed milk
> ¾ cup water
> 2 teaspoons vanilla extract
> 1½ cups heavy cream

In a medium bowl, combine the sweetened condensed milk, water, and vanilla; mix well. In a large bowl, beat the heavy cream until soft peaks form. Stir the sweetened condensed milk mixture into the whipped cream until well blended. Cover and freeze for 2 hours. Remove from the freezer and stir until smooth. Cover and freeze overnight, or until firm, before serving.

***Note:*** For a truly perfect dessert, top a scoop of this with some Soda Fountain Hot Fudge (page 156). Mmm, mmm!

# No-Bake
# Baked Alaska

Extravagance was the word for the 1980s. And what dessert is considered more extravagant than Baked Alaska? Looking at this one on the cover, you'd think it was difficult and time-consuming to make. Uh-uh! This version is easy—and rich, too!

  1 package (19.8 ounces) brownie mix, batter prepared according
     to the package directions
  ½ gallon strawberry ice cream, slightly softened
  1 container (8 ounces) frozen whipped topping, thawed
  ½ cup sweetened flaked coconut, toasted

Bake the brownies according to the package directions for an 8-inch round cake pan. Remove from the pan and allow to cool completely. Meanwhile, line an 8-inch bowl with plastic wrap; pack with the strawberry ice cream. Cover and freeze until firm. Place the prepared brownie on a platter and invert the molded ice cream onto it. Remove the plastic wrap. Spread the whipped topping over the ice cream and the sides of the brownie, then sprinkle with the coconut. Freeze for at least 2 hours, or until firm. Serve, or cover and keep frozen until ready to serve.

***Note:*** To remove the ice cream from the bowl easily, use the warmth of your hands or some warm water to heat up the bowl slightly; then the ice cream should come right out. And since this Baked Alaska doesn't require any final baking, it can easily be made in advance and kept frozen until ready to serve.

# Strawberry Snowballs

Ice cream novelties sure have a personality all their own . . . and this one's an "oldie but goodie" that you're gonna want to share.

   2 cups sweetened flaked coconut
   1 package (4-serving size) strawberry-flavored gelatin
   1 quart vanilla ice cream

Line a baking sheet with waxed paper. In a resealable plastic storage bag, combine the coconut and dry gelatin. Close the bag and shake until the coconut is completely colored; place in a shallow dish. Scoop the ice cream into 6 balls and roll each in the coconut mixture. Place on the baking sheet, cover loosely, and freeze until firm. Serve, or cover well and keep frozen until ready to serve.

***Note:*** You've heard the expression "as many colors as the rainbow." Well, the same applies here, since these can be made in as many colors as there are gelatin colors.

# Good Fortune Sherbet

## about 2 quarts

Don't think you have to go hunting for that ice cream machine buried somewhere in your cabinet. Not for this one! It's a favorite anytime, but a classic dessert to complete a Chinese dinner . . . and boy, is it an easy throw-together!

    1 package (4-serving size) orange-flavored gelatin
    1 cup boiling water
    1 cup orange juice
    1 can (11 ounces) mandarin oranges, drained
    1 container (8 ounces) frozen whipped topping, thawed

In a medium bowl, combine the gelatin and boiling water; stir until the gelatin is dissolved. Add the orange juice; mix well. Cover and chill until slightly thickened. Add the mandarin oranges and beat until well combined and the oranges are broken up. Add the whipped topping and beat just until well combined. Cover and freeze for at least 4 hours, or until firm, before serving.

*Note:* If this is frozen solid, remove it from the freezer a few minutes before serving to thaw slightly.

# Old-fashioned Tortoni

Tortoni is a traditional Italian-American dessert that combines vanilla ice cream with crushed almonds or coconut. Here's my version—a tasty tribute to the original.

> 1 pint vanilla ice cream, softened
> 12 maraschino cherries, chopped
> 1½ cups frozen whipped topping, thawed
> ¼ cup sweetened cocoa
> ½ cup crumbled coconut macaroons (see Note)

Line a 6-cup muffin tin with paper baking cups. In a large bowl, combine the ice cream and cherries; mix well and scoop into the baking cups. Place in the freezer until firm. In a medium bowl, combine the whipped topping and cocoa; mix well and spoon over the ice cream mixture. Top each with crumbled macaroons. Cover and freeze for at least 2 hours, or until firm, before serving in the paper cups.

***Note:*** No macaroons on hand? No problem—just substitute ½ cup toasted coconut.

# Frozen Chocolate-Coconut Mounds

Just as nutty-yummy as those almond candy bars that became popular in the '40s and '50s, these frozen treats are the perfect sweet ending to any trip down memory lane.

>   6 chocolate wafer cookies
>   1 pint vanilla ice cream, slightly softened
>   1 cup sweetened flaked coconut
>   2 tablespoons chopped almonds
>   ⅓ cup chocolate-flavored hard-shell topping

Line a 6-cup muffin tin with paper baking cups; place a chocolate wafer cookie in each cup. In a large bowl, combine the ice cream and coconut; mix well. Using an ice cream scoop, place a rounded scoop of the ice cream mixture in each cup. Top each with the chopped almonds and freeze for 1 hour, or until firm. Drizzle each with the hard-shell topping until the tops are completely covered. Freeze until the chocolate shells are firm. Serve, or cover and keep frozen until ready to serve.

***Note:*** Another favorite version of this is to mix chopped miniature peanut butter cups with the ice cream, then sprinkle with chopped peanuts and top with a chocolate—peanut butter-flavored hard-shell topping.

# Simple Peach Melba

## 6 servings

Groovy! Cool! Peachy keen! After you say all those, you'll still be wondering how something so simple can be so heavenly. It's just a combination of canned fruit and jam, but it sure does make ice cream stand out!

> 1 can (29 ounces) peach halves, drained
> 6 dessert shells (see Note)
> 1 quart vanilla ice cream
> 1/3 cup raspberry preserves, melted

Place 1 peach half cut side up in each dessert shell. Scoop the ice cream equally over the peach halves. Spoon the raspberry preserves over the ice cream and serve immediately.

***Note:*** Dessert shells can be found in the produce or bakery department of the supermarket. Since the number of peach halves in a can varies, you may have a few extra—just serve them on the side or save for another use. You know, this is also great served over slices of pound cake instead of in dessert shells.

# Coffee Bavarian Crème

These days, going out to eat at a restaurant is a lot more common than it was years ago. With our busy schedules, moms and dads don't have the time to cook a complete meal every night—but that wasn't always the case. I remember the days when restaurant dining was only for special occasions like birthdays and anniversaries. Know what the best part of that was? Fancy desserts like this one!

2 tablespoons unflavored gelatin
½ cup sugar
¼ cup instant coffee granules
2½ cups boiling water
1 cup cold water
1 teaspoon vanilla extract
1 cup frozen whipped topping, thawed

In a large bowl, combine the gelatin, sugar, and coffee granules with the boiling water; stir until well mixed and dissolved. Add the cold water and vanilla; mix well. Chill for about 1 hour, or until slightly thickened. Beat until light and fluffy, then add the whipped topping and continue beating until well combined. Pour into a gelatin mold or serving bowl. Cover and chill for at least 4 hours, or until firm. Unmold and serve, or keep chilled until ready to serve.

***Note:*** Grab a grater and a chocolate bar and that's all you need to make the perfect topper.

# Apple-Raisin Tarts

---

## *6 servings*

---

When TV dinners first hit the market, they offered a sweet baked apple dessert that was served bubbling hot. I've come up with a version that works whether you're finishing off a quick dinner in front of the TV or a fancy holiday meal!

> 2 tablespoons butter
> 1 can (20 ounces) sliced apples, drained (see Note)
> ½ cup packed light brown sugar
> ¼ cup golden raisins
> ¾ teaspoon ground cinnamon, divided
> 6 single-serve graham cracker tart shells
> ½ cup heavy cream
> 1 tablespoon granulated sugar

Melt the butter in a large skillet over medium heat. Add the apples, brown sugar, raisins, and ½ teaspoon cinnamon and cook for 2 to 4 minutes, or until the sugar is melted and the sauce is thick. Spoon into the tart shells; cover and chill for at least 2 hours. In a small bowl, beat the heavy cream, granulated sugar, and the remaining ¼ teaspoon cinnamon until stiff peaks form. Spoon over the tarts and serve, or cover loosely and keep chilled until ready to serve.

*Note:* This can also be made with fresh apples. Simply peel and thinly slice 2 to 3 apples, then cook in the brown sugar mixture until tender.

# Blueberry Betty

The key to making the best dessert Betty around? Use fresh bread cubes. And these days, with our no-fuss bread machines, it takes very little "dough" to make fresh bread for using in all sorts of goodies!

 2 pints blueberries, washed
 ⅓ cup sugar
 1 tablespoon cornstarch
 ½ loaf French bread, cut into ½-inch cubes (about 4 cups)
 ½ cup (1 stick) butter, melted
 ½ teaspoon ground cinnamon

Preheat the oven to 375°F. Coat an 8-inch square baking dish with nonstick cooking spray. In a large bowl, combine the blueberries, sugar, and cornstarch; toss to coat. Add the bread cubes and melted butter; mix well. Spoon into the baking dish and sprinkle with the cinnamon. Bake for 35 to 40 minutes, or until bubbly and the bread is golden. Serve warm.

***Note:*** For a totally awesome dessert, serve this with fresh whipped cream made simply by beating 1 cup (½ pint) heavy cream with 2 to 3 tablespoons confectioners' sugar until stiff peaks form.

# Apricot Bread Pudding

## 4 to 6 servings

Let's count down the hits to the number one favorite part of a meal—dessert! This bread pudding combines the comfort tastes of yesterday with the ease of today.

8 slices white bread, torn into large pieces
1 can (15 ounces) apricots, drained and coarsely chopped
2 cups milk
2 eggs, beaten
¼ cup (½ stick) butter, melted
½ cup sugar

Preheat the oven to 350°F. Coat an 8-inch square baking dish with nonstick cooking spray. In the baking dish, combine the bread pieces and apricots. In a large bowl, combine the remaining ingredients; mix well and pour over the bread mixture. Bake for 55 to 60 minutes, or until golden and set. Serve immediately, or allow to cool, then cover and keep chilled. Serve warm or chilled.

## Did You Know . . .
A loaf of bread cost about 14¢ in 1950?

# Cherry-Pineapple Crumb Cobbler

In the 1950s and '60s, cake mixes and pie fillings were the main ingredients in many desserts. Sure, they make things easier, but they taste good, too—and that's what's important in *my* kitchen.

> 1 can (20 ounces) pineapple rings, drained
> 1 container (20 ounces) cherry pie filling
> 1 package (18¼ ounces) yellow cake mix
> ½ cup (1 stick) butter, cut into pats

Preheat the oven to 350°F. Coat a 9" × 13" baking dish with nonstick cooking spray. Place the pineapple rings in the bottom of the baking dish. Spoon the cherry pie filling over the top and sprinkle with the dry cake mix. Top with the pats of butter and bake for 30 to 35 minutes, or until golden brown. Allow to cool slightly and serve warm.

***Note:*** Don't forget to top this with a scoop or two of creamy vanilla ice cream.

# Soda Fountain Hot Fudge

Whether we stopped there on the way to a sock hop or after the drive-in, the soda fountain was always the place we could go to find the perfect hot fudge. Who knew then that it'd be a memory-making taste?!

    1 can (14 ounces) sweetened condensed milk
    2 squares (1 ounce each) unsweetened chocolate
    ⅛ teaspoon salt

In a small saucepan, combine all the ingredients over low heat. Heat until warm and the chocolate is melted, stirring frequently. Serve warm.

*Note:* Use as a topping for ice cream, cheesecake, or any favorite dessert. Store any leftovers in a tightly sealed jar in the refrigerator, then just remove the lid and rewarm in a microwave or saucepan before serving.

# Be-boppin' Beverages

Icy Orange Limeade                          159
Strawberry Spritzer                         160
Very Cherry Cola                            161
Ultimate Root Beer Float                    162
Spiced Iced Tea                             163
Sweet 'n' Creamy Iced Coffee                164
Company-Fancy Italian Coffee                165
Steamin' Hot Chocolate                      166
Mile-High Chocolate Malted                  167
Very-Berry Strawberry Milk Shake            168
Peachy Orange Smoothie                      169
Rise 'n' Shine Bloody Mary                  170

# Icy Orange Limeade

Orange limeade equals pure sparkling refreshment. Take it from me, a pitcher of this timeless taste will quench the heartiest thirsts!

    1 can (6 ounces) frozen limeade, thawed slightly
    1 cup orange juice
    1 bottle (1 liter) chilled ginger ale

In a large pitcher, combine all the ingredients; mix well and serve over ice.

***Note:*** To give this even more zest, add orange and lime slices to the pitcher and garnish each serving with an additional slice.

# Strawberry Spritzer

*about 1½ quarts; 4 to 6 servings*

When we were kids, most of us sipped on kiddie cocktails or Shirley Temples to pretend we were like the grown-ups. Now that we *are* grown up, we'll sip on strawberry spritzers. That's 'cause we all still have a little bit of kid in us.

> 1 bottle (1 liter) chilled seltzer water
> ¾ cup strawberry-flavored syrup (see Note, page 168)
> 6 strawberries, washed and split partway from bottom

In a pitcher, combine the seltzer and strawberry syrup; mix well. Fill six glasses half full with ice and place a strawberry on the rim of each glass. Pour an equal amount of the seltzer mixture into each glass. Serve immediately.

***Note:*** Make your own tasty straws for this by cutting off both ends of strawberry licorice sticks. Now that's cool!

# Very Cherry Cola

*1 to 2 servings*

Sipping cherry cola through a paper straw sure serves up great memories of sitting at drugstore soda fountains in the '50s. Well, the old-fashioned soda fountain may be all but a thing of the past, but we can make our own cherry cola today in just minutes.

    ¼ cup grenadine syrup or maraschino cherry juice
    1 can (12 ounces) chilled cola

Pour the grenadine syrup into a large glass, then add the cola and stir until well combined. Add ice, if desired.

## Did You Know . . .
Cola is used in lots of dishes, from roasts to cakes?
It adds really rich flavor.

# Ultimate Root Beer Float

Okay, I need you to burn one, take it through the garden, and pin a rose on it. While you're at it, don't forget the frog sticks and a fifty-five. Would you believe that's diner lingo for a hamburger with lettuce and onion, French fries, and a root beer? And you say you want ice cream in your root beer? That makes it a fifty-five with a bottom.

   1 quart vanilla ice cream, slightly softened
   ½ cup finely crushed root beer barrel candy
      (about 18 candies)
   2 bottles (1 liter each) chilled root beer soda

Line a rimmed baking sheet with waxed paper. In a medium bowl, combine the ice cream and candy; mix well. Shape into 6 well-rounded scoops and place on the baking sheet. Freeze until firm, or until ready to use. Fill six tall glasses or mugs three-quarters full with root beer and top each with a scoop of the ice cream mixture. Serve immediately, with straws.

***Note:*** Make sure to not overfill the glasses with the root beer, because you'll need room for the foam that forms when you add the ice cream.

# Spiced Iced Tea

Flavored teas are really "in" today! And there's no need to go out and buy pricey ready-made ones, since we can brew them fresh with our favorite flavorings for pennies a serving!

 3 cups apple juice
 2 cups cranberry juice
 2 cups water
 ⅓ cup sugar
 3 tea bags
 1 orange, cut in half
 2 cinnamon sticks

In a soup pot, combine all the ingredients; bring to a boil over high heat. Reduce the heat to low and simmer for 20 minutes. Remove and discard the tea bags, orange, and cinnamon sticks. Allow to cool, then refrigerate. Serve chilled over ice.

**Note:** You might want to save the cinnamon sticks and use them (plus a few more) to garnish the glasses.

# Sweet 'n' Creamy Iced Coffee

Take a break from serving your usual iced tea and serve iced coffee—'cause coffee is really "hot" these days. The sweetened condensed milk in here gives it just the right sweet creaminess, so forget about hitting one of those fancy coffee shops. Serve this over ice cubes for a number one homemade refresher!

⅔ cup instant coffee granules
6 cups hot water
1 can (14 ounces) sweetened condensed milk

In a heat-proof pitcher, dissolve the coffee granules in the hot water. Add the sweetened condensed milk; mix well. Allow to cool slightly, then serve in tall glasses over ice.

***Note:*** Top each serving with a dollop of whipped cream (canned is fine) and a few chocolate sprinkles.

# Company-Fancy Italian Coffee

Italian families have been enjoying cappuccino and other specialty coffee drinks since long before there were coffee bars on nearly every American street corner. Know what? We don't need an expensive machine to make this quick-and-easy version of cappuccino.

> 3 cups hot strong black coffee
> 1 cup milk
> 1 tablespoon light brown sugar
> ⅓ cup frozen whipped topping, thawed
> Ground cinnamon for sprinkling

In a large saucepan, combine the coffee and milk and heat over medium-high heat until simmering. Moisten the rims of 4 to 6 coffee mugs with water. Place the brown sugar in a shallow dish and dip the mug rims in the sugar. Fill the mugs with the coffee mixture and top with the whipped topping and a sprinkle of cinnamon. Serve immediately.

***Note:*** To really dress these up, serve in glass coffee mugs or stemmed glasses, top each with a dollop of real whipped cream (canned is fine), and serve with the rock candy sticks that double as stirrer and sweetener.

# Steamin' Hot Chocolate

## about 1 quart; 4 to 6 servings

Put away those envelopes of instant hot cocoa and get ready to enjoy this sensational sipper that's made from scratch. It may take a few extra minutes, but trust me, it's worth it.

½ cup sugar
¼ cup unsweetened cocoa
4 cups whole milk, divided
½ teaspoon vanilla extract

In a large saucepan, combine the sugar, cocoa, and 1 cup milk over medium heat; bring to a boil, stirring constantly. Add the remaining 3 cups milk and the vanilla; bring to a boil, stirring occasionally. Pour into individual mugs and serve warm.

**Note:** To complete the authentic hot chocolate experience, top each serving with a generous dollop of whipped cream and some shaved chocolate.

# Mile-High Chocolate Malted

Very often, a familiar aroma or taste brings happy memories flooding back to us. For me, it's a sip of a chocolate malted that takes me back to my childhood neighborhood soda fountain. It's tastes like this that make us feel good all over again.

> 3 large scoops vanilla ice cream (about 1 pint)
> 1½ cups milk
> 1 bag (7 ounces) chocolate malted milk balls,
>     crushed (see Note)

In a blender, combine all the ingredients and blend on high speed until thoroughly mixed. Pour into tall glasses and serve immediately.

***Note:*** Here's an easy way to crush the malted milk balls: Place them in a resealable plastic storage bag, close tightly, and crush with a rolling pin or hammer. You know, you can use whole, 2%, 1%, or fat-free milk—the choice is yours. And to really lighten it up, use low-fat frozen yogurt in place of the vanilla ice cream.

# Very-Berry Strawberry Milk Shake

*about 1½ quarts; 4 to 6 servings*

Whether we're watching the Spice Girls or Jerry Lee Lewis, there's bound to be a "whole lotta shakin' goin' on" when we serve up these thick, fruity refreshers!

1 quart strawberry ice cream
1 pint strawberries, washed and hulled
2 cups (1 pint) half-and-half
¼ cup strawberry-flavored syrup (see Note)

In a blender, combine all the ingredients and blend on high speed until smooth and thick, occasionally scraping down the sides of the blender, if necessary. Serve immediately in tall glasses and don't forget to add the fun—you know, the straws!

**Note:** Strawberry syrup is usually found near the ice cream in the supermarket, with the other toppings and syrups. It's fun to top each milk shake with a dollop of whipped cream and a whole strawberry.

# Peachy Orange Smoothie

Smoothies became popular in the '70s, along with health foods. Back then, we could only find them in specialty stores, but these days, smoothie shops are sprouting up all over—and even our supermarkets sell ready-to-drink smoothies in the refrigerator section. So now that you know all the places you can get yummy smoothies, how 'bout adding your kitchen to the list?! All it takes is a blender and you're ready to go!

      2 cups orange juice
      1 package (20 ounces) frozen sliced peaches
      3 tablespoons honey

In a blender, combine all the ingredients; blend until smooth and thick. Serve immediately.

***Note:*** Want to make a real treat for a Sunday brunch? Add about ¾ cup peach schnapps to make these into frozen "fuzzy navels" (for adults only, of course).

# Rise 'n' Shine Bloody Mary

*about 2 quarts; 6 to 8 servings*

No need to dig out the bitters and hot sauce like we did in yesteryear. Now we can make this easy eye-opener as fast as 1–2–3.

> 6 cups Bloody Mary mix
> ¾ cup vodka or tequila
> 2 tablespoons fresh lemon juice
> ¼ teaspoon black pepper

In a large pitcher, combine all the ingredients; mix well. Serve over ice.

**Note:** For a spicier Bloody Mary, add some prepared white horseradish and/or hot pepper sauce. And don't forget to add a rib of celery to each glass for stirring.

Index

all-wrapped-up garlic bread, 41
almond toffee brownies, 139
*American Bandstand,* 74
American cheese, in Mom's cheese
    melts, 42
American chicken chow mein, 58
antipasto, memory lane, 8
anytime deviled eggs, 9
appetizers, 1–11
    anytime deviled eggs, 9
    creamy fruit cup, 11
    crispy crunchy pita chips, 5
    grilled vegetables with onion
        dip, 3
    mash 'em, smash 'em guacamole, 4
    memory lane antipasto, 8
    party pâté, 6
    rockin' rollin' cheese ball, 7
    sweet-and-sour wings, 10
apple(s):
    in creamy fruit cup, 11
    pork chops, 73
    -raisin tarts, 152
apple jelly, in glazed baby
    carrots, 99
applesauce:
    in easy-crust custard pie, 137
    in roast pork in a bag, 75
apricot bread pudding, 154
Arby's, 18
artichoke hearts:
    in Italian veggie toss, 23
    in memory lane antipasto, 8
asparagus, lemon-chive, 93
avocados, in mash 'em, smash 'em
    guacamole, 4

backyard bean bake, 94
bacon, in diner-style liver and onions,
    72
bacon bits:
    in backyard bean bake, 94
    in "baked" potato salad, 30
    in onion ring salad, 18
    in refrigerator layered salad, 22
    in wow-'em cheese fries, 112
baked Alaska, no-bake, 145
"baked" potato salad, 30
bananas, in creamy fruit cup, 11
bean bake, backyard, 94
bean sprouts, in American chicken
    chow mein, 58
béarnaise sauce mix, in saucy brussels
    sprouts, 98
beef:
    in chili sauce, 45
    family spaghetti and meatballs, 69
    liver and onions, diner-style, 72
    Mom's pot roast, 68
    simmerin' Swiss steak, 70
    "souper" burgers, 43
    stew-pendous goulash, 71
    TV dinner meat loaf, 67
beefed-up chili sauce, 45
beer dogs, bubblin', 44
beets, tangy Harvard, 96
bell peppers, *see* green peppers; red
    peppers; yellow peppers
beverages, 157–170
    company-fancy Italian coffee, 165
    icy orange limeade, 159
    mile-high chocolate malted, 167
    peachy orange smoothie, 169

rise 'n' shine Bloody Mary, 170
soda fountain hot fudge, 156
spiced iced tea, 163
steamin' hot chocolate, 166
strawberry spritzer, 160
sweet 'n' creamy iced coffee, 164
ultimate root beer float, 162
very-berry strawberry milk shake, 168
very cherry cola, 161
biscuits, crispy buttery, 37
black olives:
    in memory lane antipasto, 8
    in veggie-packed pizza, 46
Bloody Mary, rise 'n' shine, 170
blueberry Betty, 153
boastin' roastin' turkey breast, 62
Boston cream pie, 135
bread pudding, apricot, 154
breads, 33, 35–41
    all-wrapped-up garlic, 41
    crispy buttery biscuits, 37
    muffin tin cloverleaf rolls, 35
    old-time corn bread muffins, 39
    oniony finger, 40
    Parmesan garlic rolls, 36
    sour cream muffins, 38
breakfast, 48–49
    stack-'em-up chocolate chip pancakes, 48
    walnut maple syrup, 49
broccoli with mock hollandaise, 97
brownies, almond toffee, 139
brussels sprouts, saucy, 98
bubblin' beer dogs, 44
Burger King, 18
burgers, "souper," 43
buttermilk-fried fish, 81

cabbage, in old-fashioned coleslaw, 28
Caesar dressing, in onion ring salad, 18

cakes:
    chocolate polka-dot, 133
    chocolate-raspberry cheese, 134
    daffodil, 129
    lemon meringue, 131
    shortcut German chocolate, 130
    sour cream coffee, 132
carrot(s):
    in chicken potpie, 60
    glazed baby, 99
    in Mom's pot roast, 68
    and pineapple mold, 29
    salad, crazy, 27
    in stew-pendous goulash, 71
    sweet peas and, 100
    in take-out-style veggie fried rice, 123
    in vegetable cornucopia, 106
    in wedged salad, 20
cauliflower, light 'n' cheesy, 101
celery:
    in American chicken chow mein, 58
    in confetti zucchini salad, 24
    in voilà vichyssoise, 16
Cheddar cheese:
    in creamy potatoes au gratin, 109
    in home-style macaroni and, 119
    in light 'n' cheesy cauliflower, 101
    in picture perfect noodle ring, 121
    rice bake, 125
Cheerios, 37
cheese:
    American, in Mom's cheese melts, 42
    ball, rockin' rollin', 7
    melts, Mom's, 42
    processed spread, in rockin' rollin' cheese ball, 7
    Swiss, in refrigerator layered salad, 22

cheese (*continued*)
    *see also* Cheddar cheese; cream
        cheese; mozzarella cheese;
        Parmesan cheese
Cheez Whiz, in wow-'em cheese fries,
    112
cherry-pineapple crumb cobbler, 155
chicken:
    chow mein, American, 58
    classic scalloped, 57
    farm-style, 54
    fried, one and only, 56
    garlic roasted, 55
    herbed, 53
    à la king, 59
    in party pâté, 6
    potpie, 60
    sweet-and-sour wings, 10
chili, beefed-up, sauce, 45
Chinese:
    good fortune sherbet, 147
    sweet-and-sour wings, 10
    take-out-style veggie fried rice,
        123
    velvety corn soup, 17
chocolate:
    in almond toffee brownies, 139
    in Boston cream pie, 135
    cake, shortcut German, 130
    chip pancakes, stack-'em-up, 48
    -coconut mounds, frozen, 149
    in half-moon cookies, 141
    malted, mile-high, 167
    in M&M drop cookies, 140
    polka-dot cake, 133
    -raspberry cheesecake, 134
    in soda fountain hot fudge, 156
    steamin' hot, 166
chop-chop salad, 21
chopped chicken liver, 6

Clark, Dick, 74
classic scalloped chicken, 57
classic tuna noodle bake, 84
cod, in buttermilk-fried fish, 81
coffee:
    Bavarian crème, 151
    cake, sour cream, 132
    company-fancy Italian, 165
    iced, sweet 'n' creamy, 164
coleslaw, old-fashioned, 28
company-fancy Italian coffee, 165
confetti zucchini salad, 24
cookies:
    cornflake, 142
    half-moon, 141
    M&M drop, 140
corn:
    on the cob, spicy lime, 102
    soup, velvety, 17
corn bread:
    muffins, old-time, 39
    stuffing in not-stuffed "stuffed"
        salmon, 88
cornflake cookies, 142
crabmeat, imitation, in shortcut lobster
    Newburg, 85
cranberries, dried, in surprise gravy, 63
crazy carrot salad, 27
cream(y):
    fruit cup, 11
    of pimiento soup, 15
    potatoes au gratin, 109
cream, heavy:
    in chicken à la king, 59
    in party pâté, 6
cream cheese:
    in broccoli with mock hollandaise,
        97
    in chocolate-raspberry cheesecake,
        134

in creamy fruit cup, 11
in rockin' rollin' cheese ball, 7
crispy:
  buttery biscuits, 37
  crunchy pita chips, 5
cucumbers:
  in chop-chop salad, 21
  salad, crunchy, 26
  seeding of, 21
  in timeless garden salad, 25

daffodil cake, 129
desserts, 127–148
  almond toffee brownies, 139
  apple-raisin tarts, 152
  apricot bread pudding, 154
  blueberry Betty, 153
  Boston cream pie, 135
  cherry-pineapple crumb cobbler, 155
  chocolate polka-dot cake, 133
  chocolate-raspberry cheesecake, 134
  coffee Bavarian crème, 151
  cornflake cookies, 142
  daffodil cake, 129
  easy-crust custard pie, 137
  frozen chocolate-coconut mounds, 149
  good fortune sherbet, 147
  half-moon cookies, 141
  lemon meringue cake, 131
  M&M drop cookies, 140
  no-bake baked Alaska, 145
  old-fashioned tortoni, 148
  peanut butter pie, 138
  pure and simple vanilla ice cream, 144
  shortcut German chocolate cake, 130
  show-off glazed doughnuts, 143
  simple peach Melba, 150
  sour cream coffee cake, 132

strawberry-rhubarb pie, 136
strawberry snowballs, 146
diner-style liver and onions, 72
dip, onion, 3
doughnuts, show-off glazed, 143
dressing, zippy corn bread, 126
dressings, salad:
  for chop-chop salad, 21
  French vinaigrette, 31
  for tomato-lover's salad, 19
  for wedged salad, 20
  *see also* salads, salad dressings

easy-crust custard pie, 137
eggplant, in lamb kebabs, 77
eggs:
  anytime deviled, 9
  in broccoli with mock hollandaise, 97
  in memory-making homemade noodles, 117
  in old-time corn bread muffins, 39
  in oniony finger bread, 40
  in our own fish sticks, 82
  in party pâté, 6
  in picture perfect noodle ring, 121
  in salmon croquettes, 87
  in sour cream muffins, 38
  in special spaetzle, 118
  in stack-'em-up chocolate chip pancakes, 48
  in tiny taters, 113
  in velvety corn soup, 17

family spaghetti and meatballs, 69
farm-style chicken, 54
fast-and-cheap browned noodles, 120
fast food, 18
fast tartar sauce, 83

fish and shellfish, 79–89
  buttermilk-fried, 81
  classic tuna noodle bake, 84
  macadamia-crusted mahimahi, 86
  not-stuffed "stuffed" salmon, 88
  our own fish sticks, 82
  perfect fried shrimp, 89
  salmon croquettes, 87
  shortcut lobster Newburg, 85
French-fried onions:
  in backyard bean bake, 94
  in onion ring salad, 18
  in veggie-packed pizza, 46
French fries, wow-'em cheese, 112
French vinaigrette, 31
frozen chocolate-coconut mounds,
  149
fruit:
  cup, creamy, 11
  *see also specific fruits*
"fuzzy navels," 169

garlic:
  bread, all-wrapped-up, 41
  roasted chicken, 55
gelatin:
  in carrot and pineapple mold, 29
  in pineapple baked ham, 76
glazed baby carrots, 99
good fortune sherbet, 147
goulash, stew-pendous, 71
gravy, surprise, 63
green beans, pearlized, 95
green peppers:
  in chicken à la king, 59
  in family spaghetti and meatballs,
   69
  in farm-style chicken, 54
  in grilled vegetables with onion
   dip, 3

in lamb kebabs, 77
in old-fashioned coleslaw, 28
grilled vegetables with onion dip, 3
guacamole, mash 'em, smash
  'em, 4

haddock, in buttermilk-fried fish, 81
half-and-half:
  in special creamed spinach, 103
  in voilà vichyssoise, 16
half-moon cookies, 141
ham:
  in memory lane antipasto, 8
  pineapple baked, 76
  in veal birds, 78
herbed chicken, 53
hollandaise, mock, 97
homemade pizza sauce, 46
home-style macaroni and cheese, 119
horseradish, white:
  in Mom's pot roast, 68
  in wedged salad, 20
hot dogs, in bubblin' beer dogs, 44

iceberg lettuce:
  in crazy carrot salad, 27
  in memory lane antipasto, 8
  in refrigerator layered salad, 22
  in timeless garden salad, 25
  in wedged salad, 20
ice cream:
  in frozen chocolate-coconut
   mounds, 149
  in mile-high chocolate malted, 167
  in no-bake baked Alaska, 145
  in old-fashioned tortoni, 148
  in simple peach Melba, 150
  in strawberry snowballs, 146
  in ultimate root beer float, 162
  vanilla, pure and simple, 144

in very-berry strawberry milk shake,
168
icy orange limeade, 159
Italian dressing:
in confetti zucchini salad, 24
in Italian veggie toss, 23
in lamb kebabs, 77
in memory lane antipasto, 8
Italian veggie toss, 23

Jacuzzi, 55
Jell-O, 29

Kentucky Fried Chicken, 18
ketchup:
in beefed-up chili sauce, 45
in old-time corn bread muffins, 39
in picture perfect noodle ring, 121
in TV dinner meat loaf, 67

lamb kebabs, 77
*Leave It to Beaver,* 37
lemon:
-chive asparagus, 93
meringue cake, 131
lettuce, iceberg, *see* iceberg lettuce
light 'n' cheesy cauliflower, 101
lime, corn on the cob, spicy, 102
lobster bisque, in shortcut lobster
Newburg, 85

macadamia-crusted mahimahi, 86
macaroni and cheese, homemade, 119
McDonald's, 18
mahimahi, macadamia-crusted, 86
main dishes:
American chicken chow mein, 58
apple pork chops, 73
buttermilk-fried fish, 81
chicken à la king, 59

chicken pot pie, 60
classic scalloped chicken, 57
classic tuna noodle bake, 84
diner-style liver and onions, 72
family spaghetti and meatballs, 69
farm-style chicken, 54
garlic roasted chicken, 55
herbed chicken, 53
home-style macaroni and cheese, 119
lamb kebabs, 77
macadamia-crusted mahimahi, 86
Mom's pot roast, 68
not-stuffed "stuffed" salmon, 88
one and only fried chicken, 56
our own fish sticks, 82
perfect fried shrimp, 89
pineapple baked ham, 76
roast pork in a bag, 75
salmon croquettes, 87
shortcut lobster Newburg, 85
simmerin' Swiss steak, 70
stew-pendous goulash, 71
tangy roasted spareribs, 74
TV dinner meat loaf, 67
veal birds, 78
make ahead:
classic tuna noodle bake, 84
dressing for timeless garden salad, 25
dressing for wedged salad, 20
herbed chicken, 53
party pâté, 6
refrigerator layered salad, 22
velvety corn soup, 17
walnut maple syrup, 49
whipped potatoes plus, 114
M&M drop cookies, 140
maple:
syrup, walnut, 49
turkey sausages, 61
mash 'em, smash 'em guacamole, 4

mayonnaise:
    in anytime deviled eggs, 9
    in crazy carrot salad, 27
    in fast tartar sauce, 83
    in light 'n' cheesy cauliflower, 101
    in old-fashioned coleslaw, 28
    in refrigerator layered salad, 22
    in timeless garden salad, 25
meat dishes, 65–78
    apple pork chops, 73
    diner-style liver and onions, 72
    lamb kebabs, 77
    meatballs and spaghetti, family, 69
    Mom's pot roast, 68
    pineapple baked ham, 76
    roast pork in a bag, 75
    simmerin' Swiss steak, 70
    stew-pendous goulash, 71
    tangy roasted spareribs, 74
    TV dinner meat loaf, 67
    veal birds, 78
memory lane antipasto, 8
memory-making homemade noodles, 117
mile-high chocolate malted, 167
milk:
    in classic tuna noodle bake, 84
    in memory-making homemade noodles, 117
    in old-fashioned coleslaw, 28
    in oniony finger bread, 40
    in perfect fried shrimp, 89
    in piled-high mashed potatoes, 111
    in saucy brussels sprouts, 98
    in TV dinner meat loaf, 67
    in voilà vichyssoise, 16
molasses, in backyard bean bake, 94
Mom's:
    cheese melts, 42
    pot roast, 68

mozzarella cheese:
    in memory lane antipasto, 8
    in veal birds, 78
    in veggie-packed pizza, 46
muffin(s):
    old-time corn bread, 39
    sour cream, 38
    tin cloverleaf rolls, 35
mushroom gravy, in piled-high mashed potatoes, 111
mushrooms:
    in American chicken chow mein, 58
    in chicken à la king, 59
    in classic scalloped chicken, 57
    in Italian veggie toss, 23
    in refrigerator layered salad, 23
    in veggie-packed pizza, 46

Nelson, 9
Nelson, Gunnar and Matthew, 9
Nelson, Ozzie and Harriet, 9
Nelson, Ricky, 9
no-bake baked Alaska, 145
noodles, 107, 117–121
    fast-and-cheap browned, 120
    homemade, memory-making, 117
    home-style macaroni and cheese, 119
    ring, picture perfect, 121
    special spaetzle, 118
    in speedy almond rice, 124
    tuna bake, classic, 84
nothing-to-it sweet potatoes, 116
not-stuffed "stuffed" salmon, 88

old-fashioned:
    coleslaw, 28
    tortoni, 148
old-time corn bread muffins, 39
olives, black, in memory lane antipasto, 8
one and only fried chicken, 56

onions:
diner-style liver and, 72
oniony finger bread, 40
ring salad, 18
onion soup mix:
in grilled vegetables with onion
dip, 3
in onion dip, 3
in "souper" burgers, 43
in tangy roasted spareribs, 74
our own fish sticks, 82

pancakes, stack-'em-up chocolate
chip, 48
Parmesan cheese:
in all-wrapped-up garlic bread, 41
-baked tomatoes, 104
in creamy potatoes au gratin, 109
in crispy crunchy pita chips, 5
in family spaghetti and meatballs,
69
garlic rolls, 36
in zucchini and tomato bake, 105
parsnips, in whipped potatoes plus,
114
parties, theme, 7
party pâté, 6
peach(y):
Melba, simple, 150
orange smoothie, 169
peanut butter pie, 138
pearlized green beans, 95
pears, in creamy fruit cup, 11
peas:
in chicken potpie, 60
in farm-style chicken, 54
sweet, and carrots, 100
in take-out-style veggie fried rice,
123
peperoncini, in memory lane
antipasto, 8

peppers, green:
in chicken à la king, 59
in family spaghetti and meatballs,
69
in farm-style chicken, 54
in grilled vegetables with onion dip,
3
in lamb kebabs, 77
in old-fashioned coleslaw, 28
peppers, red:
in confetti zucchini salad, 24
in crunchy cucumber salad, 26
in grilled vegetables with onion dip, 3
in lamb kebabs, 77
peppers, roasted:
cream of pimiento soup, 15
in memory lane antipasto, 8
in veggie-packed pizza, 46
*see also* pimientos
peppers, yellow, in confetti zucchini
salad, 24
perch, in buttermilk-fried fish, 81
perfect fried shrimp, 89
picture perfect noodle ring, 121
pies:
Boston cream, 135
easy-crust custard, 137
peanut butter, 138
strawberry-rhubarb, 136
piled-high mashed potatoes, 111
pimientos:
in American chicken chow mein, 58
in chicken à la king, 59
in classic scalloped chicken, 57
in classic tuna noodle bake, 84
in piña colada rice, 122
soup, cream of, 15
piña colada rice, 122
pineapple:
baked ham, 76
and carrot mold, 29

pineapple (*continued*)
  -cherry crumb cobbler, 155
  in piña colada rice, 122
pita bread, in crispy crunchy pita
    chips, 5
pizza and pizza sauce, 33, 46–47
  homemade, 46
  veggie-packed, 46
Pizza Hut, 18
pork:
  chops, apple, 73
  roast, in a bag, 75
  tangy roasted spareribs, 74
potatoes, 107–114
  au gratin, creamy, 109
  in chicken potpie, 60
  in Mom's pot roast, 68
  piled-high mashed, 111
  rosemary roasted, 110
  salad, baked, 30
  in stew-pendous goulash, 71
  tiny taters, 113
  in voilà vichyssoise, 16
  whipped, plus, 114
  wow-'em cheese fries, 112
  *see also* sweet potatoes
potato flakes, in salmon croquettes, 87
potluck dinners, 30
pot roast, Mom's, 68
poultry, 51–63
  *see also* chicken; turkey
processed cheese spread, in rockin'
    rollin' cheese ball, 7
pure and simple vanilla ice cream, 144

radishes:
  in memory lane antipasto, 8
  in refrigerator layered salad, 22
raisin(s):
  -apple tarts, 152
  in crazy carrot salad, 27

red peppers:
  in confetti zucchini salad, 24
  in crunchy cucumber salad, 26
  in grilled vegetables with onion
    dip, 3
  in lamb kebabs, 77
refrigerator layered salad, 22
rhubarb, strawberry pie, 136
rice, 107, 122–125
  bake, Cheddar, 125
  piña colada, 122
  speedy almond, 124
  take-out-style veggie fried, 123
rise 'n' shine Bloody Mary, 170
roasted peppers:
  cream of pimiento soup, 15
  in memory lane antipasto, 8
  in veggie-packed pizza, 46
  *see also* pimientos
roast pork in a bag, 75
rockin' rollin' cheese ball, 7
rolls:
  muffin tin cloverleaf, 35
  Parmesan garlic, 36
romaine lettuce, in onion ring salad,
    18
rosemary roasted potatoes, 110

salads, salad dressings:
  "baked" potato, 30
  carrot and pineapple mold, 29
  chop-chop, 21
  confetti zucchini, 24
  crazy carrot, 27
  crunchy cucumber, 26
  French vinaigrette, 31
  Italian veggie toss, 23
  old-fashioned coleslaw, 28
  onion ring, 18
  refrigerator layered, 22
  timeless garden, 25

tomato-lover's, 19
wedged, 20
salami, in memory lane antipasto, 8
salmon:
  croquettes, 87
  not-stuffed "stuffed," 88
salsa:
  in mash 'em, smash 'em
    guacamole, 4
  in wow-'em cheese fries, 112
sandwiches, 33, 42–45
  bubblin' beer dogs, 44
  Mom's cheese melts, 42
  "souper" burgers, 43
*Saturday Night Fever,* 48
sauces:
  homemade pizza, 46
  mock hollandaise, 97
  tartar, fast, 83
saucy brussels sprouts, 98
sauerkraut, in tangy roasted spareribs,
  74
sherbet, good fortune, 147
shortcut:
  German chocolate cake, 130
  lobster Newburg, 85
show-off glazed doughnuts, 143
shrimp, perfect fried, 89
side dishes:
  Cheddar rice bake, 125
  creamy potatoes au gratin, 109
  fast-and-cheap browned noodles,
    120
  nothing-to-it sweet potatoes, 116
  picture perfect noodle ring, 121
  piled-high mashed potatoes, 111
  piña colada rice, 122
  rosemary roasted potatoes, 110
  skillet sweet potatoes, 115
  special spaetzle, 118
  speedy almond rice, 124

take-out-style veggie fried rice,
  123
tiny taters, 113
whipped potatoes plus, 114
wow-'em cheese fries, 112
zippy corn bread dressing, 126
*see also* vegetables
simmerin' Swiss steak, 70
simple peach Melba, 150
skillet sweet potatoes, 115
soda fountain hot fudge, 156
"souper" burgers, 43
soups, 13, 15–17
  cream of pimiento, 15
  velvety corn, 17
  voilà vichyssoise, 16
sour cream:
  in "baked" potato salad, 30
  coffee cake, 132
  crunchy cucumber salad, 26
  in grilled vegetables with onion
    dip, 3
  muffins, 38
  in oniony finger bread, 40
  in our own fish sticks, 82
  in piled-high mashed potatoes, 111
  in wedged salad, 20
  in whipped potatoes plus, 114
spaetzle, special, 118
spaghetti and meatballs, family, 69
spareribs, tangy roasted, 74
special creamed spinach, 103
speedy almond rice, 124
spiced iced tea, 163
spicy lime corn on the cob, 102
spinach, special creamed, 103
stack-'em-up chocolate chip pancakes,
  48
steak, simmerin' Swiss, 70
steamin' hot chocolate, 166
stew-pendous goulash, 71

strawberry(ies):
   in creamy fruit cup, 11
   milk shake, very-berry, 168
   -rhubarb pie, 136
   snowballs, 146
   spritzer, 160
stuffing, zippy corn bread dressing, 126
suburbs, 94
surprise gravy, 63
   in boastin' roastin' turkey breast, 62
sweet-and-sour wings, 10
sweet 'n' creamy iced coffee, 164
sweet peas and carrots, 100
sweet potatoes:
   nothing-to-it, 116
   skillet, 115
Swiss cheese, in refrigerator layered
      salad, 22
Swiss steak, simmerin', 70
syrup, walnut maple, 49

take-out-style veggie fried rice, 123
tangy:
   Harvard beets, 96
   roasted spareribs, 74
tartar sauce, fast, 83
teriyaki sauce, in sweet-and-sour
      wings, 10
theme parties:
   carrot and pineapple mold, 29
   rockin' rollin' cheese ball, 7
timeless garden salad, 25
tiny taters, 113
tomato(es):
   in chop-chop salad, 21
   in homemade pizza sauce, 46
   -lover's salad, 19
   in memory lane antipasto, 8
   in Mom's cheese melts, 42
   Parmesan-baked, 104
   in refrigerator layered salad, 22

in simmerin' Swiss steak, 70
in stew-pendous goulash, 71
in timeless garden salad, 25
and zucchini bake, 105
tortoni, old-fashioned, 148
Trader Vic's, 86
tuna noodle bake, classic, 84
turkey:
   breast, boastin' roastin', 62
   sausages, maple, 61
TV dinner meat loaf, 67

ultimate root beer float, 162

veal birds, 78
vegetables, 91–106
   broccoli with mock hollandaise, 97
   cornucopia, 106
   glazed baby carrots, 99
   grilled, with onion dip, 3
   in Italian veggie toss, 23
   lemon-chive asparagus, 93
   light 'n' cheesy cauliflower, 101
   Parmesan-baked tomatoes, 104
   pearlized green beans, 95
   saucy brussels sprouts, 98
   special creamed spinach, 103
   spicy lime corn on the cob, 102
   sweet peas and carrots, 100
   tangy Harvard beets, 96
   zucchini and tomato bake, 105
veggie-packed pizza, 46
Velcro, 55
velvety corn soup, 17
very-berry strawberry milk shake,
      168
very cherry cola, 161
vichyssoise, voilà, 16

walnut maple syrup, 49
water chestnuts:

in sweet peas and carrots, 100
in vegetable cornucopia, 106
wedged salad, 20
Wendy's, 18
whipped potatoes plus, 114
white horseradish:
in Mom's pot roast, 68
in wedged salad, 20
Worcestershire sauce, in picture
perfect noodle ring, 121
wow-'em cheese fries, 112

Xerox, 55

yellow peppers, in confetti zucchini
salad, 24
yellow squash:
in grilled vegetables with onion dip, 3
in vegetable cornucopia, 106

zippy corn bread dressing, 126
zucchini:
in grilled vegetables with onion
dip, 3
salad, confetti, 24
and tomato bake, 105
in vegetable cornucopia, 106

# Mr. Food®'s Library Gives You More Ways to Say. . . "OOH IT'S SO GOOD!!®"

WILLIAM MORROW

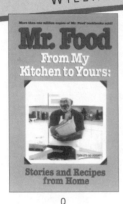

Q

R

S

T

U

V

W

X

Y

Z

AA

# Mr. Food® CAN HELP YOU BE A KITCHEN HERO!

Let **Mr. Food**® make your life easier with Quick, No-Fuss Recipes and Helpful Kitchen Tips for

**Family Dinners • Soups and Salads • Potluck Dishes • Barbecues • Special Brunches • Unbelievable Desserts**

### . . . and that's just the beginning!

Complete your **Mr. Food**® cookbook library today. It's so simple to share in all the *"OOH IT'S SO GOOD!!®"*

✂-------------------------------------------------------------

| TITLE | PRICE | | QUANTITY | | |
|---|---|---|---|---|---|
| A. **Mr. Food**® Cooks Like Mama | @ $14.95 each | x | _____ | = | $_____ |
| B. The **Mr. Food**® Cookbook, *OOH IT'S SO GOOD!!*® | @ $14.95 each | x | _____ | = | $_____ |
| C. **Mr. Food**® Cooks Chicken | @ $ 9.95 each | x | _____ | = | $_____ |
| D. **Mr. Food**® Cooks Pasta | @ $11.95 each | x | _____ | = | $_____ |
| E. **Mr. Food**® Makes Dessert | @ $ 9.95 each | x | _____ | = | $_____ |
| F. **Mr. Food**® Cooks Real American | @ $14.95 each | x | _____ | = | $_____ |
| G. **Mr. Food**®'s Favorite Cookies | @ $11.95 each | x | _____ | = | $_____ |
| H. **Mr. Food**®'s Quick and Easy Side Dishes | @ $11.95 each | x | _____ | = | $_____ |
| I. **Mr. Food**® Grills It All in a Snap | @ $11.95 each | x | _____ | = | $_____ |
| J. **Mr. Food**®'s Fun Kitchen Tips and Shortcuts (and Recipes, Too!) | @ $11.95 each | x | _____ | = | $_____ |
| K. **Mr. Food**®'s Old World Cooking Made Easy | @ $14.95 each | x | _____ | = | $_____ |
| L. "Help, **Mr. Food**®! Company's Coming!" | @ $14.95 each | x | _____ | = | $_____ |
| M. **Mr. Food**® Pizza 1-2-3 | @ $12.00 each | x | _____ | = | $_____ |
| N. **Mr. Food**® Meat Around the Table | @ $12.00 each | x | _____ | = | $_____ |
| O. **Mr. Food**® Simply Chocolate | @ $12.00 each | x | _____ | = | $_____ |
| P. **Mr. Food**® A Little Lighter | @ $14.95 each | x | _____ | = | $_____ |
| Q. **Mr. Food**® From My Kitchen to Yours: Stories and Recipes from Home | @ $14.95 each | x | _____ | = | $_____ |
| R. **Mr. Food**® Easy Tex-Mex | @ $11.95 each | x | _____ | = | $_____ |
| S. **Mr. Food**® One Pot, One Meal | @ $11.95 each | x | _____ | = | $_____ |
| T. **Mr. Food**® Cool Cravings: Easy Chilled and Frozen Desserts | @ $11.95 each | x | _____ | = | $_____ |
| U. **Mr. Food**®'s Italian Kitchen | @ $14.95 each | x | _____ | = | $_____ |
| V. **Mr. Food**®'s Simple Southern Favorites | @ $14.95 each | x | _____ | = | $_____ |
| W. A **Mr. Food**® Christmas: Homemade and Hassle-Free | @ $19.95 each | x | _____ | = | $_____ |
| X. **Mr. Food**® Cooking by the Calendar | @ $14.95 each | x | _____ | = | $_____ |
| Y. **Mr. Food**®'s Meals in Minutes | @ $14.95 each | x | _____ | = | $_____ |
| Z. **Mr. Food**®'s Good Times, Good Food Cookbook | @ $14.95 each | x | _____ | = | $_____ |
| A A. **Mr. Food**®'s Restaurant Favorites | @ $14.95 each | x | _____ | = | $_____ |

**Send payment to:**
**Mr. Food**®
P.O. Box 9227
Coral Springs, FL 33075-9227

**Book Total** $_____

+ Postage & Handling for *First Copy* $ **4.00**

+ $1 Postage & Handling for Ea. Add'l. Copy
(Canadian Orders Add Add'l. $2.00 *Per Copy*) $_____

Name _____

Street _____ Apt._____

**Subtotal** $_____

City _____ State_____ Zip_____

BKZ1

Add 6% Sales Tax
(FL Residents Only) $_____

Method of Payment Enclosed: ☐ Check ☐ Money Order

Please allow up to 6 weeks for delivery.

**Total in U.S. Funds** $_____